SPOTLIGHT GUIDE TO
ANGLING
IN THE SOUTH-WEST

MIKE MILLMAN

D1784291

Lynton
Combe Martin
Minehead
Dunster
Watchet
Brue
Bridgwater

SOMERSET

Tone

Taw
Parrett

DEVON

Otter

DORSET

Exe
Exeter
Lyme Regis
Bridport
Piddle
Teign
Starcross
Sidmouth
West Bay
Exmouth
Abbotsbury
Dorchester
Frome
Dawlish
Teignmouth
Chesil Beach
Weymouth
Dart
Tor Bay
Portland Bill
Dartmouth
Brixham
Kingswear
Slapton
Salcombe
Start Point

BRITISH BROADCASTING CORPORATION

Published by the
British Broadcasting Corporation
35 Marylebone High Street
London W1M 4AA

ISBN 563 17890 6
First published 1981
© Mike Millman 1981

Printed in England by
Whitstable Litho Ltd, Whitstable, Kent

CONTENTS

INTRODUCTION

The South-west is an anglers' paradise, and that applies as much to the trout, salmon and coarse-fishing enthusiasts as to the sea angler who is after such species as shark, conger and pollack.

This guide sets out to provide information on the best places to fish, freshwater licence requirements, charter boatmen for deep-sea, and inshore fishing, self-drive dinghy hire, and weather forecasts.

The details are the result of practical experience and association with the area's top anglers over two decades.

Spotlight Guide to Angling provides a short cut to finding consistent rod and line sport at almost any point in four counties.

Have good fishing!
Mike Millman

SEA FISHING

Cast a baited hook into salt water at almost any spot around the coastline of the South-west, and there is a good chance it will be picked up by a hungry fish. Most species common to the British Isles are enticed into the lower English Channel by the arm of the Gulf Stream, which encourages rapid growth at all levels of marine life.

If you have the ambition to become the holder of a British Record the opportunities here are much greater than anywhere else, a statement confirmed by a look at the record list issued by the National Anglers Council Fish Committee, to whom all claims must be sent.

Secretary is Peter Tombleson, 5 Cowgate, Peterborough PE1 1LR. Telephone: Peterborough 54084. The Council issue a free booklet containing the rules of procedure that must be followed to the letter.

Shore Fishing

Our sea-fishing journey around the South-west begins in Dorset, a county with a fascinating coastline of great contrast. An angler basing himself on the bustling holiday town of Weymouth has a tremendous variety of marks and species to fish for.

Roughly twelve miles from the town to the east is **Durdle Door**, which gets its name from a natural fault in the rock face. It's generally regarded as one of the best areas for shore fishing in the county and among heavyweights caught in recent years are double-figure bass and bull-huss, conger getting close to 50 lb, wrasse of 6 lb 3 oz and super mullet, a species which hunts the ground in large numbers.

Durdle has a stony steeply-shelving beach, and a bait cast 50 yards will end up 30 ft below the surface at half-tide up. Hidden rocky outcrops present the usual hazards, but as legering is far and away the most rewarding method, tackle losses must be tolerated. Very light float gear baited with bread, a tiny piece of

Rough fishing from rocks on Cornwall's North coast.

mackerel flesh, or coarse fishing maggots is the way to attract the mullet, but ground baiting with bread and water mix is essential. Although daytime fishing can be rewarding, an after dark session is more likely to produce a catch of conger and bass.

There are reasonable car-parking facilities above the beach, which is reached by a steep path and stone steps. **Ringstead Bay** is a shingle beach backed by Dorset's famous white cliffs. The best fishing is at the eastern end, which means a fair walk, so don't take more tackle than you really need. Local anglers concentrate most of their efforts near a World War II concrete gun emplacement, and among the species to be expected are bass, black bream, wrasse, mackerel, garfish, pollack and conger. In the winter, whiting and cod put in an appearance, and are fished for with sand-eel, squid and mackerel strip, lug and ragworm. Legering is the principal method.

An offshore reef running for quite a way, parallel to the beach, contributes much to the quality of the fishing. Masses of seaweed comes ashore when the wind blows strongly from the southerly quarter, and makes life difficult, if not impossible. **Osmington Mills** is another of the Weymouth area's topshore fishing venues, and it has a reputation for producing large conger, and plenty of them, even during daylight, which is somewhat unusual. Be warned, the ground is a nightmare of rock and weed, so sandbag sinkers instead of expensive lead will do much for your pocket. There are car-parking facilities at the mills and a bus service operates at regular intervals from Weymouth. Telephone Weymouth 783645 for details. **Redcliff beach** and cove has a tremendous reputation for all the species mentioned so far, to which can be added thornback ray, often taken in double figures on crab and fish baits. It can only be reached from **Bowleaze Cove**, where there are car-parking facilities.

Weymouth has a long stone pier, which gives full protection to the busy harbour. Many species, among them pollack, bass, mackerel, wrasse and flatties, are caught during the day, but night fishing is far more likely to result in a worthwhile catch. Float fishing is very popular, particularly for pollack, many fish weighing 2 lb and over being taken on king-rag or ragworm. Conger are fished for on the outer edge, and large specimens have been taken on legered squid and mackerel offered on an 8/0 hook to a short trace of heavy-duty nylon monofilament. Spinning and feathering for mackerel are good methods for making reasonable bags, particularly in the early morning when the tide is coming in. This type of fishing is best avoided when large numbers of summer visitors are about.

Mullet fishing has always enjoyed a fine reputation at Weymouth. Two small jetties that run out from the main pier make ideal stations for chasing this fascinating and often infuriating fish. The lightest of floats, a couple of small split shot to cock it, a size 6 hook tipped with bread or mackerel flesh, and you're in business. Ground baiting is a must.

Not long ago the stone pier was the setting for a world record when Robin Bray fished nonstop for fifteen days and nights. His final tally of weighable fish over a laid down minimum size was 39, topped by a bass of just under 7 lb.

Weymouth tackle shops sell a variety of fresh baits but if you prefer to collect your own lugworm, try low tide at Castle Cove, The Fleet or Weymouth Sands. White rag can also be found at these places, but not in quantity. Red ragworm can be dug at Sidney Hall Corner, in the harbour. The ground under Nothe Fort will yield crabs and limpets, and prawns can be taken with a baited 'throwout' or a conventional push type net. Live prawn is a great bait locally and accounts for more large bass than all other types put together.

Portland Bill is a peninsula and a pretty rugged one at that. The sea is doing its best to erode the landscape, and an average of 0.3 metres is lost annually. Large portions of undermined cliff have fallen into the sea, and many more pieces are in the process of going, so great care must be exercised when fishing from the ledges.

Much of the terrain is rough enough to require mountaineering experience, but for brave souls, sport is nothing short of superb. Of the many species taken from Portland's rocky ledges the conger is the most spectacular. Specimens of 60 lb have been caught at night and 40-pounders are common. Other fish taken in quantity at the 'Bill' include bass and pollack to double figures and there is first-class mullet fishing. A specimen of 10 lb 1 oz caught just offshore has held the British Record since 1952. Among more accessible places to fish on Portland are **Grove Point**, **Church Ope Cove** and **Godnor**. The area is fully detailed on Ordnance Survey sheet No. 194.

Running west from Portland to West Bay is the eighteen-mile-long **Chesil Beach**, said to be the longest stretch of shingle bank in the world. Its popularity with beach-fishing enthusiasts is great, most of the top catches being made on winter nights.

A sought-after species is cod, which has been caught to a weight of 30 lb; it would be wrong to give the impression that fish of this size are plentiful, but every year sees at least a dozen landed in the heavyweight class. To those can be added hundreds of lesser fish including many in double figures. Whiting feature strongly in winter catches. Usual baits are squid, mackerel and all types of marine worms, but lugworm in particular. Tackle rigs are usually 2-hook paternosters or single-hook legers. Spurdogs are a common catch and being a predator that isn't fussy what it eats, almost any bait takes them. Many specimens up to the British Record weight of 16 lb 12 oz are caught at night which is certainly the best time to make a good bag. Among true heavyweight species hunting Chesil's surf are tope and conger. Tales of massive eels breaking away after protracted battles are legion, some of them true. One of the most exciting things in sea fishing is the sight of a huge eel lashing in anger at the water's edge under the light cast by a good pressure lamp.

Getting a 40-pounder safely onto the shingle can only be done with a long-handled gaff, but those with screw-in heads should be avoided, as most eels spin, which can all too easily detach the hook.

A conventional 12-ft beachcaster, 4/0 multiplier loaded with 35-lb breaking strain monofilament to a short wire trace, and 8/0 hook, is the right tackle. The rig is fished as a running leger, the weight simply being run onto the reel line.

Among the most popular marks are **Chesil Cove**, which is right under Portland, and **Abbotsbury Beach**, roughly halfway along the Chesil, where marvellous catches of spurdog, bullhuss, tope, bass and conger have been made.

Between the land and the bank near **Chickerell** is the Fleet, a stretch of water that is often calm, when a huge and unfishable surf is pounding the open shore a hundred yards away. Among the species present are bass, flounder, dabs and silver eels. Lugworm, ragworm and peeler crab are the principal baits for bottom fishing.

Bridport

West Bay. The twin stone and steel-faced breakwaters which create the canal like entrance to West Bay's small harbour also mark the Western end of the Chesil Beach.

The best catches are made after dark on a rising tide with springs seeming to have a slight edge. Bottom fishing is almost exclusively the method used, sand-eels, rag or lugworm, peeler and soft-back crabs taking several species of flatfish, bass, pollack, spurdog and pouting. At dusk during the summer months spinning at the top of the tide is rewarding for mackerel and garfish. Good bags can be made with the lightest of spinning rods and a small skirted spool reel loaded with 6-lb breaking strain monofilament to a small metal lure. Feather traces are successful, but the sporting level is nothing by comparison.

The Dorset coast has a big population of conger, and many large fish fall to shore anglers. Night fishing with squid or mackerel baits mounted on a 6/0 hook to a short wire trace has resulted in many memorable battles. The local record for the species stands in the 60-lb class. The same method often picks up spurdog, which also run big in the area, during the winter months. Cod and good whiting feature strongly in catches at this time of the year.

During southerly gales, huge waves march in from the open bay to break with tremendous force on the beach and stonework. In these conditions it is simply asking for trouble to fish from the heads of either pier. Bait is not easy to come by on this wild stretch of shingle coast, so it is best if you bring a supply with you. West Bay has a tackle shop right on the harbour, run by Lawrie Rathbone, who will be pleased to give details for membership of the West Bay Sea Angling Society.

Lyme Regis

The Dorset holiday town lies at the head of a steep wooded valley. Its small but picturesque harbour is protected from southerly gales, which can be severe, by a complex of stone piers. A detached breakwater known as North Wall gives shelter from south-easterly blows. When the wind is anything over force five from either direction heavy seas smash onto stonework. They are majestic to watch, but also dangerous so caution should be uppermost in mind when these conditions exist.

Bass fishing is often very good during the flood tide with the best catches coming from dusk on, although early morning sessions have also proved their worth. A single hook rig baited with sand-eel, peeler, soft-back crab, or bunched lugworm is the usual method and baits. Sliding float fishing can be profitable an hour before to an hour after high water, but generally only takes fish in the 1- to 2-lb size range.

Bottom fishing at night during the winter with fish strip, sand-eel or lugworm attracts pouting, bull-huss and spurdog. Thornback ray are an occasional catch but should be regarded as a bonus rather than a species to be specifically fished for. Pure winter fish are whiting but it is very much a case of being there at the right time to make a good catch. Bunched lugworm offered on a short single-hook leger, or a light 2-hook paternoster are correct rigs and bait.

A good many conger are holed up in gaps in the stonework and of rough ground close by. Fish in the 20-lb class have been taken but there is little doubt that dedicated year-round fishing for them would result in much larger ones taking a gaff.

At the other end of the size scale are the mackerel which are fished for during the summer and autumn. Conventional spinners, small metal lures, and tiny artificial eels spun from the outer head which is marked by a lamp standard, will result in plenty of exciting sport. There are several local tackle shops selling a range of equipment, but bait is available only on a seasonal basis.

Lyme Regis becomes congested during the holiday season and the harbour car-park fills up very quickly. With a great many people walking on the breakwaters care must be taken when casting. There are lovely beaches of fine golden sand for the youngsters.

We now cross the border into Devon.

Sidmouth

Sidmouth has a very long shingle beach which is subject to heavy surf when the wind comes from the southern quarter. Bass are a principal quarry and fish to 11 lbs have been caught recently. The best catches are usually made at the west end where pure shingle gives way to rough terrain. Sand-eel, crab, and worm are recommended baits. Fishing during the autumn months is usually the most rewarding. Among other species regularly caught in the area are bull-huss, flounder, three bearded rockling and whiting. Dinghy fishing close inshore gives sport with whiting, plaice, dabs and turbot. A 23½-pounder taken a couple of miles out from the beach recently broke the area record for the species.

A little way to the east of Sidmouth is **Branscombe Beach** which fishes extremely well for bass during October and November. Sidmouth Sea Angling Club have played host to the Wyvern Division of the National Federation of Sea Anglers Shore Championships on numerous occasions and such is the fishing popularity of the area there are never less than 300 competitors.

Exmouth Pier

Fishing rights are owned by the Exmouth & District Angling Association who have a comfortable club-house on the pier. Day tickets are 20p senior 15p junior; obtainable between 8.30 a.m. and dusk from the club steward. Temporary membership is available for holiday anglers. The pier is on the east side of the River Exe, directly opposite the sand dunes of Dawlish Warren, and makes an excellent platform to fish for bass, pollack, wrasse, pouting and flatties. Although the general area is predominantly sandy with many bars that create hazards for small boat fishermen the ground around the pier is rough, consequently bottom fishing is hard on terminal tackle. Sliding float fishing finds success with pollack when the tide is flooding, most of the fish taking bunched ragworm. If the target fish are flatties, peeler crab is the best bait, ragworm coming a poor second.

Flounder are common during the winter months but plaice have been difficult to find in recent years, despite the fact very large fish are regularly caught from the Warren spit, which stretches quite a way out from the west side of the estuary, towards the pier head.

Fine conger have been caught in the past, but getting a real heavyweight safely onshore is not easy. Three fish between 40 and 54 lbs were taken in a single session about five years ago. Early morning and at dusk are the most productive periods for general fishing particularly in the autumn when good numbers of mackerel, garfish, and school bass come within easy reach of float and spin fishing techniques.

There are plenty of places in the estuary where soft-back and peeler crab can be found, and the mud holds good numbers of ragworm and lugworm. Prawns are common around the base of the pier and can be collected with a baited dropnet. Offered live on a light trace to float gear they get a ready response from most free swimming species.

Local tackle shops sell live bait and a wide range of tackle.

Exe to the Teign

The long stretch of South Devon coastline between **Starcross** and **Teignmouth** is one of the most popular West-country areas for family holidays. With dozens of holiday camps, caravan and camping sites situated within a stone's throw of the sea, it's no wonder that fishing is one the principal pastimes.

First, let me point out that the flood tide doesn't put any appreciable depth of water within casting range from the wooden pier or the stone wall until the second hour of the run, but you can fish into the main channel from the mixed ground of mud and shingle at any time. Flounder and school bass are frequently caught on bottom fished ragworm and lugworm in this area, and getting bait is never a problem, as half an hour's digging will produce ample for a session.

Catches during the day are not at all good, but dusk and after dark fishing is rewarding, especially when it coincides with the water coming in. The pier is the terminus for a pedestrian ferry which runs across the Exe to the busy town of Exmouth, and once on the eastern side you can fish from a more substantial pier.

Bottom fishing with medium weight end tackle, baited with crab, lug or ragworm, will take bass, plaice, dabs and flounder. If your fancy runs to something bigger, step up the tackle and leger a strip of squid or mackerel for conger.

Sliding float fishing with rag or lug is the method for pollack, but the fish seldom run more than a couple of pounds. Sandy beaches are numerous at Exmouth, and reasonable casting with leger gear will put a bait among flatties and bass.

Dawlish Warren on the west side is a long spit of land jutting across the mouth of the river, and is justly famous for plaice, flounder and dabs. Soft-back or peeler crab is the bait, but worm is a reasonable substitute. A cast of about 80 yards is needed to reach the deep-water channel running off the east end of the spit where the biggest plaice lurk.

The Warren's mile-long main beach is divided into sections by wooden groynes. Fishing during the flood tide takes plaice in the 3- to 4-lb class, but as the sand shelves very gradually, it's necessary to wade out as far as possible before casting.

Between **Dawlish** and **Teignmouth** outcrops of red sandstone and small harbours make good stations for bass fishing at night. Leger gear baited with crab is always the successful method.

Between the outcrops there are long stretches of sand where reasonable casting with crab, lug, ragworm or sand-eels will take plaice, dabs, flounder and a few bass.

Teignmouth itself needs no introduction as a sea-angling centre. Fishing from the beach with bottom gear is great for plaice, flounder and bass, but the biggest flats are caught between October and March, on peeler and soft crab. The tidal Teign is probably the best flounder river to be found anywhere. Winter sport gets going in October and lasts well into March, when the the fish leave for their spawning grounds in the open sea. They run to a large size and 3-pounders are regularly taken on peeler, or soft-back crab. To fish with any other bait is really a waste of time.

The **Shaldon** side of the river offers the best chance for easy fishing, as there are many accessible paths leading down to small beaches, but car-parking presents a few problems.

A very good spot, about a mile downstream from the long bridge, which is a popular platform in its own right, is **Coombe Cellars**, complete with a handy pub right at the water's edge, and unlimited car space. Here you can fish from the beach, or the wooden jetty. Fishing is best during the flood tide and many flounder are caught during springs. Most of the Teign's regulars use two-handed spinning rods, or light beachcasters and multipliers, as fairly long casting is needed to put a bait into the deepwater channels where the biggest specimens are found.

A running leger, or a paternoster with two snoods to size 1 longshanked hooks and a flat lead is right for the end gear. Hungry bait-robbing crabs can be a menace, but you can beat them by incorporating a small float into the trace close to the hook, which lifts the bait just out of their reach.

Ordnance Survey sheet No. 192.1:50,000 series covers the area in fine detail.

Torbay

This great holiday area has a wealth of shore fishing. The most popular and rewarding mark is **Hopes Nose**, which can easily be reached from the famous Marine Drive. A huge range of species has been caught across the years, many fish becoming West-country records.

Much sought after are outsize wrasse, and fish of 7 lb are taken on bottom fished peeler and soft crab. Float fishing also pays off, but doesn't pick up the real heavyweights. Fish baits have little effect, so time spent getting crab is more than justified. Large mullet are all around the nose, most of the specimen fish coming from the area where a sewer outfalls into the sea.

Just to the right of the main area are a group of rocks renowned for large conger and several fish over 40 lb have been taken at night on mackerel or squid. It's very hard on tackle so be sure to have plenty of traces and weights. Fishing these rocks is not for the nervous, as a gap of about 6 ft has to be jumped. The sound of water rushing into a great cavern hollowed out over the years, some 20 ft beneath your feet, doesn't help either.

Black bream are frequently caught on float and bottom baits, some topping 3 lb. The best time to fish for them is in the autumn and early winter. Quality bass can always be expected and there is no finer way of attracting them than a lively sand-eel, or prawn offered on float tackle.

The heaviest fish recorded is a beauty weighing over 12 lb, but larger ones have been lost. Between Hopes Nose and Torquay Harbour there are several good places, among them **Meadfoot slipway** and **Meadfoot Beach**. Pollack, bass, mackerel and garfish can be caught by spinning during the early morning and late evening. Conger are numerous in the area, but it is essential to fish after dark. A flood tide gives the best results. Britain's record shore conger of 69 lb was caught close by, at a mark known as **Natural Arch**, but the floor of the old quarry is difficult to reach. In Torquay harbour are **Haldon** and **Princess Piers**, both very popular for bottom and float fishing. Evening sport with mackerel can be good during the summer and autumn.

Crab and worm baits take flounder, dabs and the occasional plaice. Mullet are everywhere in the harbour area, but they are difficult to catch from the piers. Fishing for them from the stone harbour wall is much better but you still need the lightest tackle and approach. **Livermead Beach** can't be fished during the day due to holiday-makers, but very early morning bass sessions can be recommended. Just recently 29 fish to a weight of 6 lb 15 oz were taken on live sand-eel by four anglers in a matter of four hours.

If you have the ambition to tangle with a big conger, then head for **Brixham's** near 1000-yard-long breakwater. Night fishing is steady throughout the year, but sport on frosty winter nights is often superb, and more than one 50-lb-plus eel has come fighting out of the depths. The number of conger hiding in caverns hollowed out at the base of the structure is generally considered to be large, a fact that occasionally induces commercial fishermen to put a long-line down, and make an easy killing. This justifiably raises the wrath of rod and line enthusiasts in the area, who are conscious of how long it takes for the stock to recover.

Many outsize eels are found close to the oil fuelling jetty, on the harbour side where the wall slopes gently down to the water, which considerably helps the landing of a big fish. Although it is unnecessary to cast more than 30 yards, tackle for record-busting conger usually consists of heavy beachcasters capable of lobbing up to 8 oz of lead and a hefty bait of mackerel or squid.

The rod's length is a great help in playing out a big fish, and also keeps the reel line well clear of the stonework in the last stage of the fight. A good multiplier filled with 30–35-lb breaking strain monofilament is absolutely essential for rough and tough congering, as the bale arm on even a large fixed spool reel is not 'man enough' for the task of bringing in 6 ft of writhing eel. The business end of the rig is an 18-in. swivelled wire trace and an 8/0 – 10/0 O'Shaughnessy hook, fished as a running leger. This pattern has a wide gape and offset point, which is much the best for carrying a big bait and taking a firm hold in the conger's mouth. By comparison the flat narrow gaped swivelled type of conger hook, employed by commercial long-liners, is poor when used in association with rod and line. After you feel the first bite, slack away a few feet of line, and allow plenty of time for the eel to swallow the bait. When the knocks become quite pronounced, wind in slowly until the solid weight of the fish can be felt, then strike the hook firmly home and pump like mad to lift the eel clear of the bottom. A long-handled gaff with the head firmly attached to the pole is essential for getting the eel ashore.

Go wreck fishing in deep water and you could find yourself playing a monster eel like this beauty of nearly 60 lbs.

It's not only conger that can be caught from the mark. Fine bass and pollack are frequently taken by float spinning, and bottom fishing, and if you're a patient sort, you can try to outwit the grey mullet that feed on the profusion of weed growing along the wall. Ground baiting with small pieces of oily mackerel flesh, mixed with bread, is a good way to get them into a feeding swim. When that's been achieved use ultra-fine float tackle, and avoid unnecessary movement and splashing.

Small to medium-size wrasse are plentiful on the outside of the breakwater and can easily be caught on leger tackle, baited with soft or peeler crab.

Torquay and Brixham are renowned centres for deep-water wreck fishing. Book at the harbour booths or ask for details in local tackle shops. Most sell a variety of fresh and frozen baits.

Dartmouth

Harbour walls, pontoons and earthwork quays on both sides of the River Dart offer easy shore fishing. **Dartmouth's** principal road edges the waterfront, between the high and lower ferries, which ply across the river, and fishing into deepish water is possible at any point. A big problem, however, along most of the stretch, is the vast number of small and not so small craft at their moorings, which seriously restricts casting. Angling activity is, therefore, concentrated at the Lower Ferry end, where the water is kept clear to give craft free passage to several sets of stone steps. Whilst the water in front of you may be empty, care must still be taken when casting, as the embankment is a very popular promenade for visitors during the holiday months. Hook a fish, no matter how big, and there's a good chance an interested crowd will gather in seconds.

During daylight, the most common species are pouting and small bass, both being numerous in the area. Early evening adds flounder, dabs, and the occasional plaice all being taken with single or 2-hook bottom rigs baited with ragworm, soft or peeler crab. In the high summer months, shoals of mackerel come into the river, and can often be reached with a spinner, the best times being early morning and late evening, especially when it coincides with the top of the tide.

With the arrival of winter the character of Dartmouth and its fishing undergoes a dramatic change. Gone are the crowds and many of the boats, leaving a virtually deserted embankment. The landing steps area is still favourite, mainly due to a handy shelter which can accommodate a dozen anglers in comparative comfort. Important when a cold north-easterly is coming straight down the river. Fishing is now very much better, and excellent catches of flounder are made, usually on peeler or soft-backs during the flood tide, which is usually the best for all river fishing.

Directly opposite Dartmouth is **Kingswear**, terminus for the Dart Valley Railway, which runs to Paignton. From the embankment a moderate cast will land a bait in deep water, for the species already mentioned with the added benefit of larger bass. Mullet are common in the river, and can be seen nosing around the weedy pontoons. A favourite place is the old floating reception area, formerly used by foot passengers for the railway. Ground bait will quickly draw fish into a shoal and it's then all down to ultra-light float gear, patience, as little movement as possible, and sheer fishing skill. Smallish pollack are also present in the area, and can be taken with a sliding float, and small ragworm.

Someway up the river is **Dittisham**, and directly opposite, **Greenway Quay**. Dittisham has floating pontoons that stretch a long way into the river which almost gives boat fishing conditions without the boat, from middle to tide up. Whilst there are no signs prohibiting fishing, it's impractical during the summer, when the small foot ferry is operating.

Greenway is reached by a narrow road running in from the main Paignton-Brixham highway, and is approximately a 10-minute drive from Galmpton. Evening is the best time to fish, the species being bass flounder and sometimes thornback ray. Greenway is traditionally a bottom fishing mark, but the tide runs fast during spring so a selection of flat and conc-shaped sinkers should be in the tackle bag.

300 yards downstream from the quay is the **Anchor Stone Rock**, which is marked by a beacon. This has been a famous bass mark for over a century, and many fine fish are taken on drift-lined baits, principally prawn, sand-eel and worm. At this point the river bends through a narrow gap, and is very deep, almost 14 fathoms at high tide, so the water literally pours through. Small self-drive boats can be hired at Dittisham; contact: Roy Andrews, telephone Dittisham 264.

Dartmouth has numerous tackle shops, where live bait can be

obtained during the summer. In winter it's virtually a ghost town, so bring your own. Worm can be dug in the mud along the upper stretches of the river and crabs hide under the weed-covered rocks. There is a large car-park in the centre of the town, and several smaller ones which usually become congested by 10.00 a.m. during the holiday months. Parking at Dittisham and Greenway is a problem between May and late September. Dartmouth area is detailed on Ordnance Survey sheet No. 192. 1:50,000 series.

Start Point, Slapton, Salcombe

Start Point, which is dominated by a lighthouse, is an excellent mark for the keen rock fisherman. Deep water right to your feet attracts a variety of species that can be caught by spinning, float-spinning, legering or using a sliding float. Perhaps the most prolific species is the wrasse, which grows to a large size on a diet of limpets, dog whelks, and crabs. They will take almost any bait, except fish-strip, but the use of soft or peeler crab gives the best chance of continuous action. The larger specimens go for baits right on the bottom, but this method is heavy on tackle.

Plaice, dabs, rays and the occasional turbot are caught, which is not surprising considering the closeness of that famed 'flattie' mark the Skerries Bank. To find these species it is necessary to cast onto the sandy patches between the rocks. A careful look from the cliff-top at low tide will show their position easily, especially on a sunny day.

Spinning with bright artificials is good for pollack and mack-erel, in the early morning, when 'Start' fishing is at its best. The last hour of the making tide, when it coincides with the onset of darkness, is another good period for rod bending sport. Float-fishing with live prawn is a well-tried method, and takes many of the free-swimmers, but of course you need a dropnet, and suffi-cient time to catch enough prawns.

In the early autumn, fine black bream swim close to the shoreline, and eagerly snatch at thin strips of squid fished on single-hook bottom tackle. Fish averaging 3 lb are caught each year and 4-pounders are not uncommon. The best spot for bream is in the small cove to the left of the point. A cast of around 80 yards is necessary to reach the scuddy ground so a light beachcasting outfit, or a heavy two-handed spinning rod is needed.

To reach Start Point you walk about a mile and then scramble down over rough ground to the water's edge, but the effort is well worthwhile. Close by is the ghost village of Hallsands, destroyed by a violent sea in the 1920s. The abandoned houses make a unique backcloth for a shore-fishing mark and the small beaches of golden shale and sand in front of them make ideal picnic areas.

To the east is **Slapton Sands**, used as a training ground by the Americans for the allies' invasion of Normandy in 1944. The beach shelves steeply, and long casters have no trouble finding 30 ft of water, although generally even a moderate cast will place a bait among fish, as they come in very close to the shore.

Slapton sands usually has a big surf, and anything over a force four wind from the southern quarter turns the sea into a maelstrom of white water. This can be a disadvantage as the bottom is so disturbed that baits are quickly buried or thrown back on the shingle. Slapton borders the southern edge of **Start Bay**, an area renowned for outsize turbot, plaice and dabs, and these species feature in shore catches. Although bottom fishing methods with crab, worms, sand-eel and squid strip are favoured for flatties, sliding float fishing has its devotees, who go for bass, black bream and garfish.

During the summer months these species are prolific along the beach, but for bream it's best to work close to the rocky ground near **Blackpool Sands** at the eastern end, and **Beesands** and **Hallsands** at the western boundary. The autumn is the best time for this hard-fighting species.

Spinning with bright artificials from the main beach is also practised, but I've not had much success outside of the early morning period on a rising tide when mackerel provide a good level of sport.

Nearby **Salcombe** is one of the West's main boating and fishing centres, so needs little introduction. Estuary boat fishing is great for plaice, turbot, dabs and flounder. The many coves are haunted by bass, the best baits being live sand-eel or crab. Salcombe has a special claim to fame in that the attractive gilt-head bream, a species relatively uncommon in our waters, is frequently taken up to the record weight of 6 lb 15 oz. Not far away is **Starhole Bay**, where the faint outline of the hull of the great four-masted windjammer *Herzogin Cecilie*, which went ashore in

1936, can be seen at low tide, when the rays of the sun lance through the clear water. There is reasonable rock fishing for wrasse and pollack. Small-eyed ray give added variety on occasions, and dab fishing is fair towards the back end of the year.

Bigbury Bay

It would be difficult to find a better location for a combined angling and family holiday than the **Bigbury Bay** area. Along this stretch of coastline, soaring headlands, rocky outcrops, sandy beaches and quiet estuaries offer the visitor a tremendous variety of sport for many different species.

The Bay is bordered on the eastern side by **Bolt Tail**, which is a noted mark for rock fishing. Big wrasse are all around this headland during the summer months and can be fished for with float or bottom gear. Successful baits range from crabs and worm, to limpets and razor fish, but fish-strip usually gets a poor response. In the autumn, pollack and bass move in close to the rocks and for both these fish, live prawn offered on sliding float tackle takes a lot of beating, otherwise worm and crab are good alternatives.

Conger are numerous but the stiff climb back up the cliff path makes them an unattractive proposition for all but the dedicated. Just inside the 'Tail' is picturesque **Hope Cove**, a favourite spot for holiday-makers seeking a suntrap. From here the shoreline to **Thurlestone** is rough, and good catches of wrasse are made from the outcrops known as **Woolman Point** and **Warren Point**, but reaching them involves a fair walk along the coastal path, and a clamber over rocky gullies. Shoals of mackerel are often within spinning distance of these spots and can be tempted with bright lures. To be successful it is essential to cast well beyond the breaking fish, and retrieve the lure back through them at an even pace. Thurlestone has a good beach that produces bass on the rising tide but most are caught at night on legered crab, sand-eel or squid strip when a good wind is whipping up the surf. Bull-huss are occasionally taken on fish-strip and there is always the possibility of a plump flounder or dab if you leger worm or crab.

Bantham marks the mouth of the River Avon, and is a fine spot for bass when the tide is flooding. Soft or peeler crab and prawns seem to be the best baits, but some anglers swear by a fresh sand-eel or a thin strip cut from the side of one. A half-hour raking or digging in the estuary sand at the water's edge is almost certain to produce enough for a few hours of fishing. Flounders are common in the river and can be contacted as far upstream as **Aveton Gifford**.

Bigbury itself and **Burgh Island** are next on the list. Neither really needs a lot of introduction as holiday-makers from all over Britain flock into the caravan and chalet sites each year. Long stretches of golden sand pounded by surf when the wind comes from the south and western quarters are a bass man's dream, but long casting is needed as the beach shelves very gradually and the bigger fish are in deep water.

Burgh Island is divided from the mainland by a neck of sand that dries out at low water. Although this can be crossed on foot in a few minutes, it could be fatal to try when the tide is flooding. During high-tide periods a vehicle designed to operate through water 12 ft deep carries passengers in safety. The rest of the island is surrounded by deep water, and on the south and west sides there are gullies and clefts holding depths up to 30 ft. It doesn't take much imagination to picture the species hiding in them – but they're big and always on the look-out for an easy meal. Car-parking facilities in the area are pretty good, but at the height of the summer season it's best to arrive early if you want to get a place. Bigbury Bay can be found on Ordnance Survey sheet No. 202. 1:50,000 series.

Stoke Point and Yealm

Stoke Point is one of the best rock fishing areas in the South-west, and hardly a day goes by, during the season, without a report of small-eyed ray or conger being caught there. The mark also offers excellent sport with pollack to 3 lb and smaller fish are numerous. Most fall to float gear, but they will slash at lures spun across the deep water in the early morning. Mackerel and garfish are around during the summer and bass come in to feed on the marine life after a blow has disturbed the water. Fish over 8 lb are not uncommon.

The beach to the left of the main rocks has produced many fine small-eyed ray. Most have been hooked during the dark hours on sand-eel, which has a clear lead over all other baits. Big bull-huss also become active after dark and a big helping of fresh mackerel, squid or a juicy crab is likely to be wolfed down. The heaviest huss on record at the mark scaled 15 lb 6 oz, and was taken on mackerel strip at the top of the tide. To the right of the beach is wrasse country. Deep gullies and thick kelp weed hide enormous fish which are not slow to take a hook, but many succeed in breaking away by diving into the underwater jungle. A long-handled landing net is an absolute necessity here as the rock platforms can be several feet above the water level. Conger are active at night and will go for any fish bait and crabs.

Species frequently caught in the Yealm area include bass, wrasse, mullet, flounder, conger and several types of ray. The estuary is flanked on both sides by heavy concentrations of rocks, but the eastern edge, running in from Gara Point, is quite accessible, and certainly produces the best catches of wrasse and bass. Most are caught on legered crab, or worm placed on the sandy patches between the rocks, but spinning with artificials across the making tide in the direction of the Mewstone can be deadly for bass, particularly in the early morning.

From **Season Point**, on the west side of the mouth, a 60-yard cast will put sand-eel, crabs or squid strip on to a flat sandy bottom that is the hunting ground of thornback and small-eyed ray. Throughout the winter, numerous fish scaling upwards of 10 lb are taken but some degree of dedication is needed, and night fishing is the best.

A sand bar runs across the estuary, and this is where the dinghy angler searches for ray. Generally the fish are found on the sheltered side of the banks as the tide runs strongly, so it is necessary to anchor some way ahead to ensure that single-hook leger rigs settle in the right place. Three ounces of lead is sufficient to hold bottom, except during the big spring tide period, when double this is needed. It is advisable to stick to the flat types as bombs are easily rolled across the firm sand. Slow trolling or 'whiffing' with artificials is the usual way of taking bass, and it is customary to work back and forth along the line of the submerged ridges.

Not far into the river is **Old Cellars Beach**, which offers superb wrasse fishing from the rocks and a nice sandy beach with safe swimming for the family. The fish feed quite happily on crab or worm baits, even when a bright sun lances through the clear water, showing up the bottom configuration.

The Yealm's main harbour is **Newton Ferrers**, one of the prettiest in South Devon, and a favourite anchorage for yachtsmen and dinghy fishermen. Big mullet are everywhere, and the 'grey ghosts' can be seen browsing around the weedy piles and the floating pontoons permanently moored some 30 yards out from the banks. As always with mullet they are difficult to catch, but employing ultra-light float tackle and groundbaiting with bread should produce at least a couple of fish during an early morning or late evening session.

Farther up the river, wooded slopes sweep right down to the water's edge, and there are plenty of spots to fish for ray and flounder. Sport with the latter species is very good between October and March, when the run of 2-lb-plus fish is at its peak. Most of the local anglers concentrate their efforts at **Cofflete Creek**, **Fisherman's Point**, and at **Puslinch Bridge**, the latter mark being at the extreme end of the tidal flow. Here submerged branches and rotting tree trunks make for a snaggy bottom, so it's best to take note of the danger areas at low tide. Worm or crab baits bottom fished in the deep-water channels cut by the tide find a ready response from the flatties, and the chances are you will also take a few school bass, and on occasions a much bigger fish.

Generally speaking, a flood tide is best for the Yealm and if you're trying the upper reaches of the river, allow about an hour over published tide times. The River Yealm can be found on Ordnance Survey sheet No. 201. Stoke Point is on sheet 202. 1:50,000 series.

Millbay Docks – Trinity Pier

Although the docks area has three distinct piers, and several harbour walls, to all intents and purposes fishing is confined to both sides of **Trinity Pier**. It's become one of the most popular spots for shore fishing, particularly during the winter when hundreds of flounder, plaice, dabs and bass move in. They're attracted by fish droppings and blood pouring from nets as millions of mackerel are unloaded from purse-seine trawlers which come and go around the clock.

It is nothing short of amazing that the docks Authority permit rod and line fishing to take place amidst all the commercial activity, and for a mere £7.00 a year at the time of writing. Permits are issued at the administrative offices.

It is said that every species of interest to anglers shows up here at one time or another. It is not an exaggeration – for example, a very large Mako Shark patrolled the entrance to the complex over a period of some days, and even dolphins have sported in the deep water between the piers.

Three species of mullet, thick-lipped, thin-lipped and golden grey are present and provide entertainment for much of the year. Only recently a young angler caught all three of them in a single session, which must be something of a record. Grey mullet are very common in the docks and larger fish ghost around the weedy pillars that hold up the piers, tantalisingly showing themselves for a few seconds before gently finning back into the dark water under the overhangs. Light float tackle baited with worm, bread or tiny pieces of mackerel is the correct approach. During the early winter they seem to lose some of their infuriating caution, and are somewhat easier to catch.

The most popular species is the flounder, which quickly become conditioned to feeding on the mackerel that literally pave the bottom close to the piers during the winter commercial season. As a result only a thin strip of that bait will make a catch. Bass are similarly well disposed to thin strips of mackerel and fish up to 10½ lb have been tempted with leger and sliding float rig. Bass between 3 and 4 lb are a common catch.

In late September and November, black bream move close inshore, and the docks have produced many fine specimens to 3 lb 9½ oz. Very thin strips of squid offered on float and bottom gear is usually the successful bait, with bunched worm a close second.

Strangely enough, conger are not fished for to any great extent, which is surprising as many large fish live in holes under the piers. The difficulty lies in getting even a moderate-sized fish up to the landing stage even at high tide, but there are steps to which an eel could be worked.

Millbay Docks is a two-minute drive from the centre of Plymouth, so it's the ideal place for young anglers and others without transport. A word of warning – Dock Police are likely to ask to see your permit during their routine patrols, those without one go quickly through the gates.

Plymouth Breakwater

There are few better shore-fishing marks than that mile-long structure guarding **Plymouth Sound**. Completely surrounded by deep water, it lies 2½ miles out from the harbour, and can be fished at most states of the tide, except during spring periods. Designed by John Rennie, the breakwater took 29 years to complete after the first stone was dropped in 1812. The flat top is 50 ft wide, giving away to 25-ft sloping sides, down to the water at low tide. Along the entire length of the southern edge, 100-ton blocks of concrete break up heavy winter seas, but even these huge slabs are moved by the power of the water, during southerly gales. To give continuous protection additional blocks are dropped each year from a specially constructed barge.

As one can imagine, two miles of weed-covered rocky and sandy ground attracts and holds many species, and it is quite common for ten different fish to be brought to the scales at the end of a competition. Wrasse abound, but the heavyweights are normally found on the southern side where they feed on limpets, crabs and small fish. Bottom fishing is the best way of taking them but with such rough ground, tackle losses are high, consequently sliding float gear is popular. Wrasse begins in May and continues right through to late October.

Pollack are at both ends, but the eastern gives the results, particularly on the back tide when the water runs out of the Sound at a fast pace. Spinning with artificials or float-spinning are good ways of contacting the fish. When 'floating' allow the trace to drift away with the tide, and steadily retrieve it until the worm bait is taken.

From April, thornback ray to a weight of 16 lb are found on the muddy ground along the north-facing side, most falling to single-hook leger rigs and peeler or soft-back crab baits. Good size plaice are also taken, the majority being hooked on worm or crab.

Fishing on either side of the old fort produces fair black bream, in the second half of the year. Thin strips of squid fished on paternosters with 1/0 hooks or a single-hook leger, is the right method, and will account for fish weighing up to 3½ lb.

For the mullet enthusiast, sport is often superb, but patience and ground-baiting with bread is needed to get them into a feeding mood. Ultra-light float tackle and a freshwater approach is needed for success with the craftiest of fish.

Big conger hide in rocky gullies between the stones and occasionally feed by day, but night fishing produces better sport, although it demands a long stay on the breakwater, as landing and leaving is only possible during daylight. End gear for conger should be kept simple, which means a single 6/0 to 8/0 hook to a wire trace, fished as a running leger. Squid or mackerel are the killing baits. To fish on the breakwater you need the services of a boat owner. Fortunately there are many skippers working out of Plymouth, who would be prepared to drop and collect a party at a prearranged time for a nominal fee. It is, however, essential to make arrangements well in advance.

River Tamar

The tidal Tamar is the natural boundary between Devon and Cornwall, and along its miles of shoreline are at least a hundred productive spots for shore anglers, and as many for the boat fisherman. The mouth of the river is marked by **Western Kings**, and **Cremyl battery**. The opening is narrow but the water is deep enough to allow the Royal Navy's biggest ships to pass through to the dockyard.

The rocks in the 'Kings' area justifiably have a reputation for superb fishing. Kimberley McGowan hooked a British Record pollack of 14 lb 12 oz, and the mark has given up a coalfish of 17 lb and numerous other good fish. During neap-tide periods the concrete hardstanding at Western Kings makes an ideal spot to fish for big conger at night, but be warned, it is costly on gear. As it is unnecessary to cast more than thirty yards to place the bait into 40 ft of water, a boat rod can be pressed into service, matched with a multiplier and 30 to 35-lb monofilament line to a short wire trace and an 8/0 hook.

At Cremyl, which is reached by a regular ferry service from Admiral's Hard, there is a small beach where many fine bass have ended their days. Legering during the early flood tide, with soft-back or peeler crab, is the best method, but some very good fish, and that includes 10-pounders, have been caught on king-ragworm.

Thornbacks to 16 lb are also regularly taken at this spot, but it is essential to bait with soft or peeler crabs.

A half-mile from Cremyl the river fills **Millbrook Lake**, a popular area for flounder fishing between November and March. Most of the action taking place at **Palm Rock** and **South Down**.

St John's Lake, a little further upstream, is much bigger than its title suggests, and only a few places are fished regularly. The Ballast Pond on its northern flank is worked for bass and flounder, and whiting are caught during the winter. It is best known for the large king-ragworm which can be found in the mixture of mud, shale and stones.

The Devon side of the Tamar is completely dominated by the dockyard, and out of bounds to all but employees, who find plenty of outsize conger in the crannies along the seawall.

Fishing is possible for large eels from the floating pontoons at **Wilcove**, or at nearby **Looking Glass Point**, where more than one 30-pounder has been caught. The St German's or Lynher River runs west from the main stream, and there are four fine marks; **Wearde Quay**, **Forder**, **Shillingham Point** and **Jupiter Point**, all basically flounder marks, but some bass and the occasional ray can be caught at night. The start of the flood is the best time to fish. Ragworm and lugworm can be dug along the shore and the weed-covered rocks give shelter to crabs.

The last mark of note, before the Tamar Bridge, is the small pier at **Saltash**, where conger to a weight of 45 lb have been taken. Although cod are extremely rare inshore, 20-pounders have been caught on legered crab from this point.

Whitsand Bay and Rame Head

The ten-mile stretch of coastline in **Whitsand Bay**, south-east Cornwall, has a dozen huge surf beaches divided by the rocky outcrops which become one at low tide. Separated, they each have characteristics of their own, and names to match. **Polhawn**, **Tregonhawke**, **Freathy** and **Tregantle**.

Between **Polhawn** and **Portwrinkle** the bass is king, the best fishing being found after dark on a rising tide, when the surf comes roaring in from the vast expanse of the Bay. If you fish during or just after a southerly blow your chances will be much improved, as in these conditions fish up to 12 lb have been caught. Another requirement for success is the ability to cast 100 yards, as the sand gently shelves into deep water. Most of the experts wade out as far as possible, before sending bottom tackle with crab, sand-eel or squid behind the breakers. At half-tide, the rocky outcrops stretch beyond the marching lines of surf, and a bait lobbed just 20 yards will lie in 15 ft of water. One of the best marks is the 'Grotto' which gets its name from a hollowed-out cavern made by a gout sufferer in the 1700s who wanted to take advantage of the salt air, an age-old cure for the ailment.

Whitsand Bay beaches also fish well for various species of flatfish, including, from time to time, turbot, although they're generally on the small side. Why this should be is something of a mystery, as long-lines laid at low water often account for 10-pounders.

At the east end of the Bay, the sand gives way to deep water-filled gullies, and heavy kelp weed, perfect ground for the keen rock angler. Most of the popular fish can be found in quantity, and wrasse fishing is splendid, bottom and float fishing techniques getting results. Spinning with 'flashy' artificials at first light is a good way of taking mackerel, and when you tire of this, switch over to light sliding float tackle tipped with worm.

Portwrinkle at the west end has two good beaches between heavy concentrations of rock, where bass roam at night. High cliffs have now given way to flatter ground, and access to the water is very easy. The area is popular with holiday-makers, consequently car-parking space close to the marks is at a premium, but there are public parks at Happy Valley, Tregonhawke, Tregantle and Portwrinkle.

Rame Head is renowned for its outstanding catches and is seldom out of the angling news. It's the rock angler's eldorado where great gullies cut deep into the head, many holding 25 ft of water at low tide. Masses of kelp weed, with stalks as thick as a man's finger, wave with the movement of the tide, hiding tackle-busting wrasse. Fish of 5 lb are common, 6-pounders always a possibility while crafty 7-lb-plus fish hang motionless below rock overhangs. Some with hooks still embedded in their jaws, as proof of their victory over an unlucky angler. Legering is the usual method of presenting crab or worm, the bait being lobbed onto the narrow sandy strips between the heavy outcrops of rock. If you choose to fish into the open sea, from any one of a dozen natural platforms, stick to float gear, either fixed or sliding. The slider allows any depth to be fished and enables a bait to be suspended just a few inches above the bottom.

Patient ground-baiting with bread in the deep gullies will

bring mullet on the feed, particularly when the water is reasonably calm. Ultra-light float tackle and firm but gentle playing of a hooked fish is the only way of dealing with them. Pollack respond well to floatfished king ragworm, and live prawn. The majority will weigh around a couple of pounds, but in the autumn fish close to double figures are not far away.

If you want an outsize conger, Rame Head fished after dark will provide it. Monsters of the species hide in deep holes in the rocks, but bringing a 50-pounder over the rough ground is no easy task. Fresh mackerel or squid on at least an 8/0 hook is the right terminal tackle, and the bait must be on the bottom. It's a useful dodge to use old steel nuts or stones wrapped in small squares of nylon instead of costly lead, the conger won't detect economy. To tackle the big eels after dark it's as well to devote all the night hours to it, as going up and down the steep cliff is not easy. If you do decide to give it a try on a flood tide basic requirements are a good lamp, and a torch as reserve, a large gaff, fishing bag and something warm to drink when the cold night wind comes blowing off the water. Be sure to fish where you can retreat as the tide comes in. Car-parking for Rame is provided in a field near the coastguard houses and presents no problem. The mark is close to the pretty Cornish village of Cawsand, where a couple of pubs well steeped in the tradition of smuggling days will welcome you after a day chasing the big 'uns.

Rame Head is on Ordnance Survey sheet No. 201 – line 48. Whitsand Bay is on Ordnance Survey sheet No. 201. 1:50,000 series.

Looe

There is little doubt sharks put **Looe** squarely on the angling map, the sport having its beginning around 1952, when comparatively few fish were caught. By the end of ten years, the annual numbers taken were exceeding an average of 3000. As one might imagine, sea fishing of this quality attracted sportsmen from all over Great Britain, and far beyond our shores. Today, Looe is a household name in the world of big-game angling.

While sharking is the most popular pastime, the small fishing town also provides the opportunity for the angler to meet up with many other sea fish, both big and small, as the waters off the rugged coastline are rich in marine life. This fact is well illustrated by the fine catches brought in from the reefs and wrecks during the Annual International Sea Angling Festival. For the shore angler, a multitude of marks exist within a few miles of the town, and opportunities for float fishing, legering and spinning are great.

Marks to the west of **Banjo Pier** – itself a fine place for fishing the rising tide for bass and pollack – include **Hannafore Point**, **Wallace Beach**, **Horestone Point** and **Leak Rock**. These fish well for wrasse, pollack, mackerel, garfish and conger.

A little further to the west is **Stinker Cove**, so named because of the thick kelp, which covers the bottom. Excellent catches of wrasse are made here but the rough ground takes a toll of gear.

To the east the marks include **Plaidy Beach**, **Millendreath Beach**, **Seaton** and **Downderry**. Good-sized bass are caught all along this stretch, mostly on the rising tide and at first and last light. For inshore dinghy fishermen, there are many marks within a mile of the rocky shoreline. **Looe Island**, separated from the mainland by a narrow gap through which the tide runs strongly on the springs, is a good place to troll for pollack and bass. Anchored-up fishing no more than 20 or 30 yards from the rock will yield big wrasse. After dark the ground all around the island is good for conger. Some time ago a 70-pounder was taken.

Offshore, the great underwater reefs such as **Phillips Rocks**, **Brentons**, **Hands Deeps** and the **Eddystone** provide tremendous sport for the deep-water enthusiasts. Throughout the year outsize pollack, ling, conger, cod and bream are taken. Most of these marks are within two hours of Looe, but good weather conditions are necessary for the boats to reach them. The wreck angler is well catered for, as there are dozens of rusting hulks which are regularly visited by Looe skippers.

During the summer months the area of open water beyond the Eddystone is the hunting ground of large numbers of sharks and every day as many as 25 boats leave for the grounds. Most are 'blues' weighing between 50 lb and 100 lb but the porbeagle and giant mako which can reach a weight of 500 lb are also caught. All boats operating out of Looe are fully licensed by the local authority.

Fowey

Fowey is another fine place for fishing holidays. The harbour attracts dozens of species that can be fished for from accessible walls, piers, rocks and sandy beaches. The ground running in from the harbour mouth is rugged, and the **Polruan** side in particular is popular for sliding float and bottom fishing in the deep water, where wrasse abound. Crabs are easy to come by at Fowey and these make a super bait. They're best presented sliced in half, minus the legs, and you needn't worry about size, wrasse have insatiable appetites and like a real mouthful. Limpets also make a good bait, and with large colonies clinging to the rocks, something to fish with is never a problem.

The Fowey area is also noted for its bass fishing and live prawn offered on float tackle is the best way of attracting them. Many fine fish make their way into the harbour and the plump 5-pounder is always a possibility. Prawns can be caught quite easily with a baited drop-net, or by pushing a long-handled net through the shallows, close to the rocks in the weedy areas. They should be hooked through the third segment from the tail, which ensures they stay lively and swim around in a natural manner.

Mullet are common, and can be seen nosing around close to the shore or feeding on an unwanted sandwich tossed away by a visitor. Evening sport with very light float gear baited with breadpaste or small worms can be great fun, but large harbour mullet are crafty creatures and difficult to catch.

On the other side of the river is the quiet wooded **Pont Creek**, the setting for Leo Walmsley's fascinating book *Love in the Sun*, a story of a fishing existence in the days of depression. School bass and flounders are present and can be taken on bottom gear baited with ragworm or crab. Pont is reached by a narrow path running down through the woods from above **Bodinnick**, or from the head of the creek itself. Parking facilities are limited in Pont Village.

From here the tidal stream makes its way past Bodinnick, where a small ferry plies a lively trade across the narrow stretch of deep water between the two banks. Some idea of its great depth can be gained from the fact that ocean-going freighters pass through the neck and moor at the china clay loading jetties just 300 yards upriver.

This is conger country and many fish up to 50 lb are caught at

33

night from boats and shore on mackerel and squid baits.

Once past the jetties, flounders and plaice are the main quarry and what a size they reach on a diet of sand-eels which abound in this area. The British record flounder of 5 lb 11 oz was taken here.

Most of Fowey's experts use sophisticated baited spoon rigs developed over many years, and these account for large numbers of fine fish. Less experienced anglers should use a single-hook leger or a 2-hook paternoster with a 6-in. snood to size 1 hook, baited with crab, worm or a thin strip of sand-eel. Sand bars run across the river near the railway sidings, and a bait offered here stands a good chance of being accepted.

Lack of space prevents a detailed look at the multitude of marks for deep-water boat fishing outside the Fowey's mouth, but suffice it to say they're renowned. If you have the chance spend a day over the **Cannis Rock** in the company of a local boatman – it will be a never-to-be-forgotten trip. The Fowey area is on Ordance Survey sheet No. 200. 1:50,000 series.

Mevagissey

Mevagissey with its colourful houses clinging to the side of steep hills, overlooking a bustling harbour, is a typical Cornish seaside village. Its association with commercial fishing stretches back hundreds of years, but with a fleet of some 30 charter boats it has now become a principal centre for rod and line anglers keen to battle it out with fish of record-breaking size. Situated roughly at the halfway point along the south Cornish coast, Mevagissey gets the full benefit of the Gulf Stream which brings a host of species into the area.

The port has inner and outer harbours, the former completely drying out at low tide during springs. Stone breakwaters guard the outer, and make ideal platforms for shore fishing into deep water at any state of the tide. Both have been the scene of many memorable captures, several fish becoming Cornish records. With ease of access both piers are very popular places, particularly during the summer months, for anglers of all ages.

The southern breakwater with its small lighthouse offers the best opportunity for a good catch. Float fishing is a much used method for taking wrasse, and there are some very big ones in the area, pollack, mackerel, garfish and bass can also be caught by the same method. The classic story of local bass is of the young angler on holiday who purchased a cheap rod and reel and a spool of line, one hook and half a dozen worms at a local tackle shop. Half an hour later he was back at the counter cradling a 7-pounder, and innocently asking if it was good enough to win the shop's weekly prize offered for the best fish.

After dark on a flood tide, especially a spring, is the best time to expect bass, and many 5-pounders are hooked each year, but the breakwater record is a magnificent fish of 14 lb 2 oz. That giant, like a few others, went for a large mackerel bait being legered for conger, which highlights the value of offering a generous helping for the largest specimens. Superb conger hide out in the rough ground on either side of both breakwaters, and in crannies at the base of the stonework, but it is only really worthwhile fishing after dark. Landing a large eel presents considerable difficulty, and fish in double figures must be worked around to the steps on the inside edges, which can be entertaining to say the least.

Mullet and Mevagissey go together like strawberries and Cornish cream but fish that habitually haunt the harbour area are well conditioned to hustle and bustle and can pick out casually thrown-away bread, as opposed to a piece containing a hook, with uncanny accuracy. Large specimens browse on the weed growing on the stonework, but to catch them one must have infinite patience and a good supply of bread soaked in pilchard oil. Minced mackerel meat mixed with a little oil in my opinion makes a better ground bait, but it must be very fine, otherwise the fish simply feed up on the particles. Very light tackle is an absolute must, certainly line no heavier than 5-lb b/s to a size 6 hook should be used. Reasonable sized dabs, plaice and flounder are caught from time to time, usually having taken bottom fished lugworm, ragworm or crab meat.

Early morning before the crowds get about is the best time for spinning, the last two hours of the flood and the first hour of the ebb usually being the most productive periods. Small metal lures or the tiniest artificial eels, particularly the fluorescent variety, take bass, mackerel and smallish pollack. There are no fishing restrictions on the breakwaters. Car-parking at Mevagissey is adequate outside the main part of the town, but to gain a place in the park close to the harbour wall, one must arrive very early in the morning or after the crowds have departed in the late evening. Obtaining bait presents no difficulties. Mevagissey has three tackle shops right on the harbour who sell worm, live sand-eel and crabs, as well as frozen squid and mackerel.

Falmouth

The vast area of **Falmouth's** harbour has dozens of super spots for both shore and boat fishing. At the entrance is **Pendennis Point**, a rocky area holding wrasse and pollack, most of which are caught on float tackle, baited with crab, prawn or worms. Apart from crab, the same method and baits account for a good many mackerel and garfish during the summer months. Spinning with artificials is rewarding in the early morning and late evening, and there is always the chance of picking up a reasonable bass.

On the eastern side of the harbour is **St Anthony's Head** and **Zone Point**. It's a stiff climb down to the rocks but well worth the effort as many wrasse up to 6 lb are waiting to be caught. In the late autumn, black bream visit the Head, and go for thin strips of squid legered on a single hook or a 2-hook paternoster.

Trefusis Point has about a mile of rocky shoreline, and a number of sand coves. Species most frequently caught are wrasse, mackerel, pollack and bass, but ray also turn up from time to time, if you leger fish-strip or sand-eel on the clear patches.

Falmouth has **Prince of Wales Pier**, and **Custom House Quay**, which are favourite spots for holiday fishing. There are no restrictions but both are busy during the day and best avoided until the bustle dies down in the evening. Then it's float or bottom fishing for flounder, school bass, pollack and mackerel.

The River Fal runs to the north from Trunaware Point past King Harry Ferry. In addition to flounder and plaice, this is big mullet country. The fish can be seen browsing along the shore and on weed growing around redundant ocean-going tankers, which are moored together near the ferry. Mullet are most active during the second half of the flood tide, and the best rig is a freshwater float, and a size 6 hook to 4-lb monofilament. Bread-flake mixed with pilchard oil, small pieces of chopped-up rag-worm or maggots make good baits. Fine bass hunt the river and are caught by both boat and shore anglers using float, spinning and bottom fishing methods, live prawns having the edge on other baits.

Inshore boat fishing in the Falmouth area can be good and there are numerous marks to choose from. Right in the middle of the shipway off Pendennis Point, marked by a tall beacon, is **Black Rock**. Here medium-weight pollack are caught from June on, with larger fish up to double figures making an appearance in the autumn. Bass are frequently taken on artificial lures or sand-eels trolled around the bay, but for good results it's usually best for fish in the early morning. Driftlining with live prawn is another method much practised by the locals.

The ground for several hundred yards off Pendennis Point is very rough and good for wrasse. Crab, worm or prawn baits dropped on the bottom will attract them, but the sliding float is also a good method during the back tide. At night there are plenty of conger looking for a meal both on this ground and all along the shoreline from Carricknath Point to St Anthony's Head.

Carrick Roads, by which name the main tidal stream is known, branches westwards at Restronguet Point, and runs up to **Perranarworthal**. This is recognised for its grand flounder fishing and many specimen size flatties are caught each year.

The Falmouth marks are on Ordnance Survey sheet No. 204. 1:50,000 series.

Coverack

The small picturesque town of **Coverack** on the eastern flank of the Lizard Peninsula is a great centre for shore-angling adventures. Stray a mile from the harbour itself, and there's a good chance you will have a quiet cove, where the water is deep and green, all to yourself. The area is nothing less than a rock fisherman's paradise as all the popular species hunt close to the shore in water that can be thirty feet deep in the gullies, even at low tide. Festooned with thick kelp, they give shelter to huge wrasse, hanging motionless under convenient overhangs until a meal comes within range. On the rising tide bass roam over the rough ground, and many a large specimen has been fooled by a legered peeler crab, or a float fished prawn.

Coverack's harbour wall is massive in construction, with a protecting rampart, which has to take the brunt of heavy water roaring in from the nearby Manacles Reef during winter gales. Fishing from the wall is only possible an hour after the tide has started to come in, with the last two hours of the flood and the first two of the ebb generally proving the most productive periods. There is no question that early morning fishing near the top of the tide is the best of all.

Among the species to be expected between mid-June and late October are pollack, mackerel, garfish, wrasse and the occasional bass. Sliding float fishing with worm or live prawn is the most popular method, but if one is after larger fish a strip of squid or mackerel legered on a short trace is better. Grey mullet are plentiful in the Coverack area, many of them running to double figures, but very few of that size have been taken with rod and line. The wall and the old lifeboat slip are good stations to fish for them, but tackle must be very light and movement kept to a minimum.

Spinning with small copper-coloured lures when there is a good depth of water can be worthwhile for pollack, mackerel and small bass, with most of the action taking place at first light. Getting up at the crack of dawn is surely no hardship during the months of high summer, particularly in such a place as Coverack. At night, conger and bull-huss can be found, but there are problems getting them on to dry land. There is a double flight of stone steps on the inside of the breakwater, but it's a long job working a fish around to them. Going west from the slipway, the ground is very rough and offers good wrasse fishing, but to the east there is a lovely beach ideal for the family. Car-parking is adequate at Coverack and the area is detailed on Ordnance Survey sheet No. 204. 1:50,000 series.

Local stores sell line, hooks, floats and some baits. Prawns and crabs can be found in the rock pools at low tide, but if fishing time is at a premium, it's best to bring a supply with you.

Coverack is the perfect setting-off point for the famous Manacles Reef, which lies a short distance offshore. When the weather is settled it is possible to obtain the services of a local boatman, for a day or half-day excursion to the reef.

The Lizard

The Lizard is Britain's most southerly point, and the scene of

,many a shipwreck. It is a very rugged peninsula, each cove having its own unique name – **Polbream**, **Vellan Drang**, **Polpeor** and **Kynance** – all species popular with anglers make close visits to the rocks providing a high level of sport.

Big wrasse are so plentiful the local fishermen net them by the dozen for crab bait, most being taken no more than 100 yards from the rocks accessible to anglers. The best wrasse marks are to the right of the disused lifeboat slip, itself a useful spot, but sometimes roped off. Bottom fishing and float-fishing are the methods, baiting with crab, worm or limpet. Cast out on to the sandy patches between the rocks, and you may pick up a thornback, small-eyed or sandy ray, all these species being regularly taken here. Again crab is the best bait, but a fresh strip of mackerel or squid will serve.

At first and last light, mackerel and pollack are in a feeding mood. Both species run to a good size, and will strike savagely at bright lures spun a few feet below the surface. Pollack are particularly fond of live prawn, and these can be presented on light float tackle. If a marauding bass should be in the vicinity, and there are some very big specimens in these waters, he will also be tempted by live prawn. While catches of the big fellows from the shore are made occasionally, dinghy and small-boat fishermen regularly take them just a short distance off the land, so long casting ability is a distinct advantage.

Conger are most active after dark and not at all difficult to hook, but actually landing the larger fish can be something of a problem. The chosen fishing platform must be reasonably flat, and big enough to allow you to back away from the water with the fish once the gaff hook has got a firm hold. The Lizard conger spots demand a long rod, with good lifting capabilities, matched with a multiplier, a 35-lb line and strong wire trace.

There are several car-parks close by, including one right on the point, overlooking the rocks and slipway. Lizard Point is on Ordnance Survey sheet No. 203, line 12. Shops sell some tackle and bait, but to be on the safe side, it is best to bring it with you. The nearest big town is Helston, eleven miles away.

Porthleven

For the visiting angler intent on a few hours' good sport while the family pursue other forms of entertainment, **Porthleven** is just about the perfect spot. The fishing port itself has an inner and outer harbour, and a stone quay which stretches a long way outside the entrance.

Fishing with sliding float rig, baited with worm or live prawn, takes wrasse, pollack, mackerel, garfish and bass, the best catches being made in the early morning and late evening, particularly during the summer after the commercial activity of the harbour has died down.

If bass is the principal quarry, a light leger trace to a 2/0 hook carrying sand-eel, prawn or worm will probably get a satisfactory response. A popular species in the area is the grey mullet. Approach the edge of the quay with stealth, and it's almost certain you will see several feeding on the weed clinging to the wall. Ground bait, usually bread mixed with water to which a little pilchard oil has been added, will often get them into a feeding mood, but like all harbour mullet they are well conditioned to the hazards of their chosen environment, and only the lightest approach tackle-wise will bring success. Spinning with metal lures, tiny artificial eels and even feathers takes mackerel and garfish. If a big shoal of the former come along, which is not uncommon in the Porthleven harbour area, sport can be very hectic indeed. No matter how many times you do it, there is always something special about flicking a lure over a shoal of the striped tigers, and anticipating the great lunge when a fish hits it during its retrieve.

On the eastern edge of the quay the ground is much rougher and one must be prepared to lose tackle, but it quickly gives way to miles of steep shingle beach. Porthleven's surf has a justifiable reputation as the haunt of large bass. The best catches are made during the rising tide after dark on sand-eel, peeler crab, mackerel and squid, but to cope with the fall of the surf a stout beachcaster capable of lobbing 6 oz of spiked lead is essential. Tremendous ground swells are characteristic of the area, and great care must be exercised at all times. On no account should one fish along the quay, when a strong southerly wind is blowing and the water is rolling in. It's spectacular but highly dangerous and many people have lost their lives, when an unexpected freak wave snatched them from a position of apparent safety.

Porthleven is two miles from Helston, the town that guards the entrance to the Lizard Peninsula. Car-parking around Porthleven harbour is limited. A good tackle shop run by Vic Strike carries a wide range of equipment at all price ranges. Fresh bait is usually available, but a phone call a few days before you intend to fish will make certain of a supply. Porthleven is on Ordnance Survey sheet No. 203. 1:50,000 series.

Penzance to Land's End

The Penzance area has a great deal to offer. Beach fishing can be good between **Marazion** and **Eastern Green**, for bass, flounder and plaice. Those who favour casting into deep water have the town harbour wall which runs well out from the station car-park. All the popular fish come within reach and can be taken on bottom or float gear, night fishing on a rising tide getting the best results. You will need a drop net to secure the 'catch' as there are no steps.

Less than a mile away is the commercial fishing port of **Newlyn**, which has several breakwaters where one can fish for plaice, flounder, dogfish, pouting and bass. Winter is the best time to search for pollack and coalfish, the multiple catches being made with float gear, baited with worm. A variety of baits can be dug locally. **Eastern Green** beach has lugworm, and **Larrigan**, which is close to Newlyn, lug, rag and whiteworm. Local bylaws restrict digging in Penzance Harbour to south of Ross Bridge and Abbey Turning Basin.

Pedn Vounder Beach holds lugworm, ragworm and sand-eels. Daily and half-day deep-sea trips are available from Penzance harbour. Evening fishing for pollack, mackerel and conger can also be booked at local tackle shops. Take the road from Newlyn towards Land's End and there are many good places to fish.

Mousehole's Stone Pier offers easy float fishing for pollack, mackerel, garfish and wrasse. Early-morning spinning with tiny artificial sand-eels and metal lures, Dorado or Toby, can be good during the last hour to high water. Next on the list is picturesque **Lamorna Cove**, a good mullet area, where fish up to 4 lb are taken between June and early October. Bottom fishing from the stone breakwater with crab pays off for wrasse. Other species are bass and conger, but it is essential to fish after dark. Lamorna is private property so mind your P's and Q's.

Rough ground running eastwards from the cove provides stations for casting into deep green water. Wrasse abound and

41

6-pounders are common. A few miles away is the most spectacular view in all Cornwall. If you think I exaggerate, stand above the unique open-air Minack Theatre, which is built on the very edge of a soaring cliff. Below will be a sea of incredible colour so white is the sand at the bottom. The immediate coastline around **Porthcurno** gives the shore angler a hundred marks to fish from, while the beach is perfect for the long casting enthusiast, and of course, the family. Float fishing from the rocks with white or ordinary ragworm, will take bass, wrasse, mackerel, garfish and pollack, which run big in this far-flung part of Cornwall. From the beach, legered crab and sand-eel will attract bass and small-eyed ray. Turbot have also been taken from time to time in the autumn, and I recall a 5½-pounder during an early winter gale, when 4-ft-high waves that had taken the colour of steel from the sky were marching in from the ocean. Bait and small items of tackle can be purchased at a garage in the village.

The area is detailed on Ordnance Survey sheet No. 203. 1:50,000 series.

Cornwall's North Coast

Shore fishing on Cornwall's north coast has never received the credit it is due. Possibly that's because of the desire by locals and regular visiting anglers from other parts of Cornwall to keep the good things quiet, and believe me, there's a lot of truth in that. Even when big catches get 'out of the bag' the given spot is often some distance away from the exact location. Depending on which way you are travelling, **Sennen** is the first and last accessible cove in England, being less than half a mile from Land's End. It has a beach of fine and almost pure white sand, but facing the Atlantic Ocean it is subject to very heavy surf which makes a spectacular sight as it comes roaring in. These conditions are ideal for bass, and the local record stands at just over 13 lb, but much larger fish are said to have been caught in the dim past.

Every two or three years, vast shoals of grey mullet visit the Sennen area, and are traditionally fished for with seine nets worked by men of several families. The history of such activity stretches back hundreds of years, and on several occasions the haul has been as much as 20,000 lb, with individual fish weighing 15 lb, a size way above the rod record.

Sennen's harbour wall is at the southern edge of the beach, which is also the site of the lifeboat station. The boat has been launched many hundreds of times to the aid of ships in distress, off what is undoubtedly as rugged a piece of coastline as can be found anywhere. Among its famous rescues is the crew of the infamous *Torrey Canyon* whose oil devasted the south-west peninsula after she went aground on the Seven Stones Reef.

Fishing from the wall is at its best between late May and October, from mid-tide to high water, and during the first hour of the ebb, particularly during springs. Early morning, or as the light is fading, is the likely time for the greatest activity, conventional float and float spinning rigs taking pollack, mackerel, garfish and the occasional bass. Successful baits are worm, prawn, and thin strips of mackerel. Ground baiting with bread and mashed mackerel will draw mullet within range, but they are shy fish at the best of times, so don't expect to make a large bag. Small wrasse are a nuisance, but for the larger fish, who can be very entertaining fighters, the ground to the left of the wall is a good proposition, crab being far and away the best bait.

During the winter months outsize pollack hunt close to the rocks in the Land's End area, and dedicated shore anglers take many fish in the 8- to 10-lb class on big legered baits. More specimen pollack caught shore fishing come from the far west of Cornwall than the rest of Britain's coastline put together. Sennen's harbour wall is as good a place as any to try your luck.

Gift and fancy good shops in Sennen Village sell odds and ends of tackle, but for anything else including fresh bait Penzance, which is nine miles away, is the closest place. White ragworm and lugworm can be dug on the beach, while rockpools to the south of the Lifeboat Station will yield small hardback crabs and prawns, but you need a wading net. It's also possible to find razor fish near the water's edge when the tide is right out on the main beach.

Around **St Ives**, there are plenty of rock and beach marks to choose from. The coastline is a maze of coves which offer sport with pollack, wrasse, mackerel and garfish for the float fisherman, while dogfish and conger and flatties are taken by legering, or a paternoster rig.

Porthmeor, **Porthglaze** and **Pendour Cove** are close together near the village of **Zennor**. Tracks run to each of them, but one must be prepared for a climb down the cliffs, followed by a vigorous scramble over base rocks.

Spots very much closer to St Ives are **Clodgy Point** and **St Ives Head**, which lie to the west of the town. Float fishing is the popular method taking wrasse and pollack.

Bass are also taken in quantity during the winter months. Best catches are made from low water up to half tide, but it is essential to have live sand-eel or peeler crab bait. St Ives's beaches are crowded during the day in the summer, and so is the sea as the rollers are a great attraction for surfers, consequently all beach-casting activity must be after dark, and even then care is needed as some enthusiasts ride the waves at night. St Ives's tackle shops have a definitive booklet on local fishing produced by members of the St Ives Sea Angling Club. Purchase gives temporary membership of the Association for one month. Ordnance Survey sheet No. 203. 1:50,000 series covers the area.

Newquay is next on our visiting list. Among the species to be expected are bass, codling, pollack, mullet, gurnard, spurdog, several kinds of flatfish and the inevitable mackerel and garfish. Principal catches are made at rock marks on either side of the town, **Towan Head** being the most famous, but the twin stone piers that protect the harbour from huge Atlantic swells, so much a feature of the north coast, make good and safe platforms to fish from. It almost goes without saying that early morning and late evening, when there's plenty of water, gives the greatest opportunity for fishing. You miss the crowds that throng the piers on summer days, and the considerable amount of small boat traffic in and out of the harbour.

Newquay is very much a holiday town, with a host of small craft engaged in morning, afternoon and evening fishing trips, as well as traditional 'two hour' mackerel outings in the bay. Sliding float fishing, which allows a bait to swim at almost any desired depth, is the main pier and rock fishing method. The best baits for pollack, mackerel and garfish are small white rag-worm, which can be dug at local beaches. Time spent working the rock pools for live prawn, along the rough coast between Fistral and Pentire Point East, is often rewarded by a catch of pollack and bass, although summer fish will seldom weigh more than a few pounds.

Mullet are plentiful in the waters around Newquay, but few are caught from the piers during the main part of the day, although large fish can always be seen roaming along the walls. Early-morning fishing in the last hour of the flood tide and at

44

high water will yield at least a couple of fish to 2 lb, but the lightest of float tackle weighted with split shot is essential. The most successful baits are bread, flakes of mackerel, or ragworm. Ground baiting plays a vital role. One local mullet enthusiast with more years to his credit than he cares to acknowledge, has nothing less than magic in his fingers, when it comes to catching them from the harbour walls and his tally must run into thousands. Like the fish he's almost a ghost – and you have to be about mighty early to witness a rare talent with gear some experts might consider totally unsuitable for the job.

In the autumn, plaice and dabs are frequently caught after dark on bottom-fished ragworm and lugworm, which are reasonably plentiful in the Newquay area. It is not uncommon for locals to have a dozen fish – mostly dabs – in the bag at the end of a session. Spinning during the autumn also gets reasonable results, the main catches being mackerel and pollack which accept all manner of bright metal lures. The new varieties of very small artificial sand-eels should also prove their worth if catches made in test areas of Cornwall are anything to go by.

There is no question that Newquay's fishing hits a peak in the winter, when spurdog and codling come within range of the shore angler. First-class catches are made, but always at night during the biggest tides. It is very much a case of 'being there at the right time' and local enthusiasts are given to planning trips with military precision. If the tide is right at say 3.00 a.m. they're in bed early, and on the rocks just in time to tackle up before the fish start to bite. One small group, who usually fish no more than two hours at a time, always return with a host of fine bass, spurs, codling and dabs, all taken by bottom fishing methods and usually bunched lugworm.

Newquay has numerous tackle shops all stocking a tremendous range of equipment. Live bait of various types is available between May and September. Tackle dealers have up-to-date information on angling club secretaries.

Trevose Head

Trevose Head is one of the truly great marks for the shore angler but to fish here you need a head for heights. Trevose towers high above the Atlantic on Cornwall's north coast and its base is endlessly swept by huge rollers from the open ocean. To fish from the lower edges is courting disaster as every so often an outsize swell arrives unexpectedly and more than one angler has been swept away. Bottom fishing, spinning and to a lesser extent float fishing are the popular methods at the headland, which is famous for big mackerel.

Tackle up with a two-handed spinning rod, a small multiplier or fixed spool reel loaded with 10-lb breaking strain line. A swivelled bomb lead is placed on the reel line and the 4-ft trace ends in a 1/0 longshanked Aberdeen hook. A live or dead sand-eel is the best bait, and is mounted by placing the point of the hook through the fish's lower lip and nicking it into the skin of the stomach. After casting out as far as possible the eel is allowed to sink at least 10 ft below the surface and then retrieved at a steady pace. Garfish and pollack are also taken by the same method, but float fishing with worm can be used as an alternative.

An even bigger species roaming in the deep water is the tope. This fish is much sought after by the 'Mountain Men' who take them to a weight of 40 lb on bottom gear, and big fish baits. Securing a tope is not without risk, as one of the party has to claw his way down the cliff with a gaff and rope – a tactic strictly for the experts.

A somewhat easier species is the wrasse, but if you hit into a 5-lb-plus fish, and these are common, you're in for a lively time. A British record of 7 lb 10 oz was set at Trevose in 1970, but even bigger fish have been lost while being lifted up the cliff face. A simple single-hook bottom fishing rig is all you need for end tackle, but your rod matched with a multiplier filled with 35-lb line must have good lifting power.

Not far from Trevose is **Constantine Beach**, a top mark for small-eyed ray. Fishing must be done after dark and live sand-eel bait is essential for success. Bass also roam the surf and many to a weight of 10 lb and occasionally bigger are caught every year. Constantine and nearby **Mother Ivey's Beach** are among the best in the area for family outings. Trevose and Constantine are on Ordnance Survey sheet No. 200. 1:50,000 series.

The thornback ray is as much a fish for shore anglers as it is for those who go afloat in small craft, among the best places to try your luck are the Yealm, Plymouth Sound, River Dart and Cornwall's Constantine Bay.

Padstow, Boscastle, Bude

The coastline between Padstow and Bude offers a tremendous variety of places to fish. **Padstow** and **Rock** on the River Camel are good setting off points for the angler after bass, flounder, dabs and ray. A popular and very useful station is **Stepper Point**, situated on the west side of the Camel estuary, and **Trebetherick Point** on the eastern flank.

Bottom fishing on the rising tide, particularly during the early morning, and late evening, is often very good, the best catches being made when a deep swell comes sweeping in from the Atlantic, stirring up the sandy bottom.

Padstow is now Britain's porbeagle shark capital, and several boats are available for charter. Porbeagles hunt over rough ground close to the shore and most of the action takes place within a mile of soaring cliffs. Battling with a giant of the species in shallow water is an unforgettable experience, particularly if the fish happens to be of world record size like the 465-lb giant caught by George Potier who was fishing from *Lady Jayne*, a top craft skippered by Ray Provis. Another species prominent for boat anglers is the tope – they're a nuisance if one is purely after shark – but deliberately fished for with medium-weight tackle they make a great day's sport. Specimens up to 45 lb are not uncommon and I have experienced as many as ten of this size during a single trip.

Wreck fishing is also possible from Padstow, during small neap tides. Local tackle shops have all the details.

Trebarwith Strand, which is not far from Tintagel, is a spot worthy of inclusion in any fishing guide. Good bass hunt the area, the best catches being made after dark on bottom fished squid, sand-eel or crab-baits. Tintagel is as rugged a piece of coast as can be found anywhere, and fishing from the rocks yields very big wrasse. Spinning at the top of the tide can be recommended for mackerel and pollack, especially in the autumn when excellent catches are made on small metal lures, ultra-thin strips of squid, and to a lesser extent tiny PVC eels.

Just over a mile away is **Boscastle**, which is tucked away between high cliffs. The entrance to the tiny harbour from the open sea is nothing more than a gash in the rock and on rough days the antics of the sea are spectacular. The small stone breakwater is a useful spot for pollack, mackerel and garfish.

Bass also show up mostly at the top of the tide, and during the first two hours of the ebb.

The **Bude** area is very popular with holiday-makers which somewhat restricts beach fishing during the main part of the day, not that catches during that time are anything to rave about. After dark it's a different story, and one can expect fish close to double figures when the surf is really rolling in after a big blow. Fishing from Bude breakwater with bottom tackle baited with crab, squid, mackerel or worm is good when there is plenty of water.

Bideford, Appledore

We have now crossed the border into North Devon, where the geography of the coastline varies tremendously. **Bideford** sits on the River Torridge and is a thriving town with a maritime history stretching back hundreds of years.

A 700-ft-long stone bridge crosses the river and is a popular spot for flounder and bass. There's no need to cast, just drop a leger rig baited with crab or worm into the deep channels. Fishing from the quay wall can also be good when the tide is high, but activity must be restricted to evenings as there is far too much commercial activity during the day. Towards the sea is the small shipbuilding port of **Appledore**, where bass are the principal quarry, flatties coming a close second. From mid-tide up the town quay makes a good platform to fish from. By driving around a tipping area much of which has already become reclaimed land it's possible to park within easy walking distance of a very steep shingle bank from where a moderate cast will put a bait into deep water. Among the species to be expected on the rising tide are bass, flounder and dabs. This part of the river is much worked by salmon netsmen and very large fish are regularly caught during the season. Any salmon caught accidently on a bait intended for lesser species must be returned to the water. There is an unpleasant aspect of fishing from the bank, namely the smell which comes from masses of seaweed buried under sand and shingle. Shark fishing boats run out of Appledore and departure times are subject to tidal conditions, consequently some trips begin just after dawn.

Perhaps the most famous of all North Devon rock marks is

Baggy Point, where all the popular species are fished for with a high level of success. There is also the possible bonus of tope as some weighty specimens have been taken.

Ilfracombe, which faces the Bristol Channel, is North Devon's principal holiday town, and there are excellent facilities for boat and shore angling. The pier is a popular place for mackerel and garfish, bass and flatties. Mullet are common in the area, and offer very good sport. Boat fishing for tope, skate and cod is as good as can be found anywhere, most of the action taking place no more than an hour from the town quay.

Watermouth Cove became famous overnight, when a Barnstaple angler hooked a British Record coalfish of 18 lb, a super fish that wrested the honours away from the mouth of the Tamar at Plymouth.

The coastline around **Coombe Martin** is rugged by any standard, inlets and small coves backed by high cliffs abound and there is a small breakwater. Float and bottom fishing with a variety of baits will take among other species skate, pollack, bass, conger and dogfish while spinning with small lures attracts mackerel and garfish. Large mullet also frequent the area, and several fish in the 5-lb class have been caught recently.

Tucked into the folds of the steep wooded valley, in the very corner of Devon, are the twin villages of **Lynton** and **Lynmouth**. Although the area's fishing doesn't receive much publicity, reasonable catches are made by shore anglers, and there is also the opportunity to go bottom and shark fishing in the bay. Lynmouth harbour's tidal and fishing activity from the jetties is from half-tide up. A good many species frequent the rough ground, and mullet fishing can be recommended.

Although **Minehead** is a very popular resort with a major holiday camp on its doorstep, there is not a great deal for the angler. In keeping with all the places around Bridgwater Bay, the tide recedes a great distance, leaving endless tracts of sand and mud. Beachcasting with lugworm, ragworm, crab and sand-eel will take flounder, dabs and the occasional bass. When the tide makes, it comes in very fast indeed.

In contrast, nearby **Watchet** has numerous worthwhile marks and a much greater range of fish. **Bassington** and **Dunster** beaches have produced three species of ray, dogfish and reasonable conger. Fishing is best after dark when the tide is coming in. Not far away are **Steart Flats**, a vast area of soft mud and water channels. When the tide is completely out the water is over two miles from shore. It's at this point the last of Britain's mud-horse shrimp fishermen set a series of fine meshed nets on tall poles, which are covered by more than 20 ft of water at high tide. To collect the catch the men propel themselves across miles of mud lying on a wood sledge and pushing with their feet. It is probably the most fatiguing job to be found anywhere in the world, but their speed and endurance over the terrain is nothing short of amazing. Rod and line fishing for flounder, dabs and ray is possible during the last hour to the top of the tide, and the first of the back. Worm or crab are the best baits. Mullet also frequent the area, but are difficult to catch. Fossils litter the ground at Steart and I have collected five types in an hour, a pleasant diversion while waiting for the fish to bite.

Burnham-on-Sea and nearby **Weston-super-Mare** are popular resorts but neither can be said to be first-grade hunting grounds for the angler. During spring tides bass, flounder and dabs are taken on beach tackle but it's usually very slow progress. The best places to try your luck are near the light tower at Burnham, and anywhere along the Brean Down sands stretch.

Boat Fishing

Well over two hundred fully-licensed charter boats operate out of West-country ports. The principal centres for deep-water wreck angling are **Brixham**, **Plymouth** and **Mevagissey**, off which lie many rusting victims of two world wars, and violent channel storms.

If you want a giant conger, ling, pollack or coalfish ship out with any one of the top-named skippers, and you could return to port with a record-breaker. Wreck fishing is very much controlled by the tides, and it is essential to have a neap if the quarry is a bottom feeder, like conger or ling. In contrast, pollack and coalies love a fast run of water and their inclination to strike at a natural bait or an artificial eel is heightened by it. In fast tide conditions most fishiing is done on the drift, except during the hour of slack water. Drift fishing over a wreck can be hectic, and very heavy on end tackle, so always follow the skipper's instructions.

Reef angling has been a way of life in the West for over a hundred years, and no wonder with such marks as **Eddystone**,

Hands Deeps, **Phillips**, **Brentons**, the legendary **Manacles** and the **Wolf Rock** to chose from. Visit any one of them and you are almost guaranteed a great catch. It is common for as many as 12 species ranging across black and red bream, ling, pollack, conger, turbot and gurnard to come over the gunwale during a single trip. I can recall a session just three miles off Stoke Point, when no fewer than 16 types of fish lay on the bottom boards. There are many skippers who specialise in rough ground fishing, which requires techniques completely different to those used in wrecking.

Boat fishing in shallow water can also be very rewarding, particularly for bass, but the best catches are always made by the anglers using live sand-eel.

Boat Fishing Contact Points

Charter Skippers and Boat Hire

Poole

Bill Cooper .... *Neptune*	Tel: Poole 79830		
Derek Case Angling Agency			
High Street	Tel:	”	6597
Bert Fray .... *Kingfisher*	Tel:	”	6597
Alan Green .... *Enterprise*	Tel:	”	79482
'Tug Wilson .... *Ebb-Ah-Flood*	Tel:	”	70440

Weymouth

Geoff Hobson Boat Charter	Tel: Weymouth 3982		
At least 20 boats operate out of Weymouth Harbour — reef/wreck/ shark fishing. Contact: Weymouth Angling Society	Tel:	”	785032

Teignmouth

John Perry
Wreck and inshore fishing/fleet of self-drive boats. Live sand-eel always available.   Tel: Teignmouth 3033

Torquay

Numerous boats can be booked at the harbour kiosks

Dartmouth

Vic Evans .... *Sea Spray*	Tel: Brixham 513280	
Wreck fishing and Skerries Bank		
Barry Lingham .... *Jennifer Ann*	Tel: Dartmouth 3485	
Lloyd Saunders .... *Saltwind 11*	Tel: Paignton 554341	

Salcombe

Small self-drive craft can be hired from the following on an hourly, daily or weekly basis:

Edgar Cove, Island Street	Tel: Salcombe 2542
Taylor Marine Sales, White Strand	Tel: " 2328
Ian Brodie, Island Street	Tel: " 3197
Salcombe Boating Centre	
White Strand	Tel: " 2046
Ken Allen Boats	Tel: 2840 (day)
	3155 (night)

Specialist Bass Fishing

Brian Cater .... *Tudor* Tel: Salcombe 2614
With live sand-eel on weekly charter basis only

River Yealm

Len Carter Boat Hire
Fleet of self-drive boats for river and estuary fishing hourly, daily or weekly Tel: Plymouth 872210

Plymouth

Plymouth Angling Boatmen's Association 38 boats for wreck/reef fishing
Booking: Ray Parsons 6, Limerick Place, St Jude Tel: Plymouth 21722
Plymouth Sea Angling Centre, The Barbican Tel: " 69416

Looe

Shark & Deep Sea Fishing Centre
The Quay, East Looe
30 boats for shark/wreck/reef fishing Tel: Looe 2189

Fowey

Colin Tabb .... *Barbara Mary* Tel: Fowey 2314
Also hires self-drive craft for river/estuary fishing. Live sand-eels usually available

Mevagissey
Mevagissey Shark & Deep Sea Fishing
Centre. 14 boats – shark/wreck/reef   Tel: Mevagissey 3430
Mevagissey Tackle Box
10 boats available
Shark/wreck/reef fishing   Tel: "   3413

Falmouth
Sea Safari's Ltd. .... *Philanderer*
Colin Macgillivray operates out of
Helford Passage   Tel: Mawnan Smith 250711
John Badger
Fleet of self-drive craft for hire   Tel: "   "   250675

Newquay
Numerous charter boats for shark; offshore, reef fishing can be
booked at Harbour Kiosk

Padstow Rock
Clive Martin .... *Baroness*   Tel: Port Isaac 480
John Watts .... *Lady Jayne*   Tel: Trebetherick 2239
(Ray Provis: skipper)
The above boats operate daily principally for porbeagle and blue
shark. Wreck and reef fishing by arrangement

Ilfracombe
D. W. Clements .... *Excel*   Tel: Ilfracombe 63460
Shark/reef fishing

Minehead
T. Arnold .... *Minehead Angler*   Tel: Minehead 5730/4158
Alf Kosh .... *Miss Tilly*   Tel: "   2674

Weston-super-Mare
Ivor Nash .... *Weston Star*   Tel: WSM 22788

Weather & Coastguard Services

If you are on a fishing holiday in the West country and want a
detailed weather forecast, these are the numbers to ring:
Hampshire, Dorset 0703 28844   *Devon, Cornwall* 0752 42534

Main Coastguard Stations are:

Portland 0305 820441
Berry Head 08045 2156
Prawle Point 032 629444
Rame Head 0752 822239

Falmouth 0326 314481
Lizard Point 032 62944
Land's End 073 687351
Trevose Head 0841 520407
Hartland Point 02374 235

STILLWATER TROUT FISHING

It would be very difficult to find a better area for reservoir trout fishing than the South-west. Well-stocked lakes ranging in size from a few to many hundreds of acres are dotted all over the region, each one being set in beautiful surroundings.

The South-west and Wessex Water Authorities have developed thirteen first-class trout fisheries, four natural waters, where fish introduced as fry are allowed to grow on in the wild, and six mixed trout and coarse fisheries. To these can be added numerous privately owned lakes, where one is almost assured of a fine bag.

Fly-fishing is the only method allowed at the principal reservoirs, but spinning and bait fishing is possible at some of the natural waters.

Rainbow, brown and brook trout are stocked into many of the Grade 1 fisheries, but the giant Wimbleball Lake high on Exmoor has the attractive tiger trout, which fights just as well as its name suggests.

To ensure stocking levels are correctly maintained all reservoir fishermen are asked to complete a catch return, at the end of each session. Failure to comply with this request can only result in a reduction of sport. The popularity of stillwater trout fishing is growing rapidly, and thousands of new enthusiasts arrive on the banks every year. The first fish to take an offered fly usually 'hooks' most of them for life – in the West country the fishing quality of it will always be high.

DEVON

Kennick

Kennick and its associated water, **Tottiford** and **Trenchford**, are in my opinion the best of all the first-class fisheries. Situated between **Bovey Tracey** and **Moretonhampstead**, they have the advantage of low hills, and heavy woodland areas, which give a

West-country reservoirs offer superb fishing for rainbow, brown, brook and tiger trout. This fine catch was made at Siblyback Lake near Liskeard in Cornwall.

great amount of shelter no matter which way the wind is blowing. Being on high ground on the edge of Dartmoor, the annual rainfall is considerably more than at other waters, so one should always be equipped with wet-weather gear. Fine days are fantastic, and the clear sharp moorland air is something to be experienced.

Catchwise, Kennick is always at the top of the returns list, producing in excess of 11,000 rainbows, 2000 brown and close to 200 brookies every season. The water rainbow record stands at over 11 lb. In 1972 a brown trout of 14 lb was caught at Kennick, and that is still the largest of its kind to come from any English reservoir. The season is 1 April – 12 October, fishing times being one hour before sunrise to one hour after sunset, both of which are often quite beautiful.

Kennick is a bank only water, and day permits can be obtained, on a self-service basis, from the warden's hut. Bob Davison looks after the three waters and does so with considerable energy. A fly-fishing expert in his own right, he's always willing to offer advice as he goes his rounds, if he says a certain fly is taking believe him – and reap the benefit. Bob can be contacted on Bovey Tracey 833199.

Tottiford and Trenchford offer fishing in very natural surroundings. Outcrops of granite make ideal platforms for casting to reach deeper water, a decided advantage in cold weather when the fish hug the bottom.

Useful flies: Orange and Teal Missionary, Black Chenille, Black Gnat, Black Matuka, Jersey Herd, Silver Doctor.

Fernworthy

Fernworthy, a moorland water of 76 acres near Chagford, somewhat exposed to winds, which can make fishing difficult at times. The lake is stocked with rainbow, brown and brook trout, the average year's catch being about 7000 fish. A low pH has been a problem in the past, and the opening date is usually dependent on water conditions having been suitable for pre-season stocking, but the lake is always a month behind the other waters. The usual fishing times apply.

Useful flies: Black Gnat, Black Muddler, Black Matuka, Brown Muddler, Sweeney Todd, Baby Doll.

Wimbleball

A giant of a water in comparison with other Authority Fisheries. Its 374 acres is high on wild Exmoor, near Dulverton and Bampton. Wimbleball's close proximity to the motorway makes it a very popular water with Midland and Welsh anglers.

The lake was first opened for fishing in 1980, and has since proved to be one of the most productive fisheries in southern England. In the first season 20,000 rainbow, brown, brook and the very attractive tiger trout were taken, many of the fish weighing upwards of 8 lb. A stocking programme carried out over a period of two years before the opening saw nearly 100,000 trout introduced into the reservoir, all of them small fish. On a very rich diet of worms and other forms of life from good land being slowly covered by the rising water they put on weight rapidly, and developed all the characteristics of truly wild fish.

The lake is now regularly stocked with trout of all sizes, but the head of original fish is likely to provide marvellous sport for the next four years at least. Wimbleball is so big there is no chance of fish being stocked out now, falling quickly to an offered fly, as is often the case at smaller reservoirs, consequently they have time to become crafty, and when hooked put up a memorable fight.

The lake's facilities are first class, and include a fleet of boats which can be booked in advance, or by self-service, when you arrive. Fishing times are identical to all other waters – one hour before sunrise to one hour after sunset, but the season is 1 May to 30 November. Two wardens look after your interests, Jim Wilson, telephone: Brompton Regis 209, and Brian Poole.
Useful flies: Black Gnat, Black Matuka, Black Muddler, Orange lure, Green Nymph, Yellow Chenille, Baby Doll, Missionary.

Wistlandpound

Wistlandpound serves anglers living in the Barnstaple, South Molton and Ilfracombe areas. It is a small but pleasant water of 41 acres, with a good head of rainbow, brown and brook trout. The average catch per rod day is 1.9, which is somewhat higher than at many other reservoirs. The year's total is usually near

6000 fish, some of them being very close to double figures.

The season is 1 April to 12 October, fishing times one hour before sunrise to one hour after sunset. Bank fishing only. Warden is Gordon Rogers, telephone: South Molton 2429.
Useful flies: Black lures, Pheasant-tail Nymph, Baby Doll, Black Matuka, Orange Muddler.

Upper and Lower Slade
Natural Trout Fisheries

Two very small waters of 4 and 6 acres – Upper and Lower Slade – near Ilfracombe. Traditional fly-fishing for rainbow and brown trout between 15 March and 12 October, sunrise to one hour after sunset.

Bag limit is three fish over 10 in. Lower Slade also has a good head of stocked coarse fish. Roger Bickly is warden for both waters. Telephone: Ilfracombe 62870.

Stafford Moor

A superb privately owned 14-acre water three miles from Winkleigh stocked with rainbow and brown trout to a weight well in excess of 10 lb. Average size of fish caught is also high at 2 lb. **Stafford Moor** is in quiet woodland with plenty of well-planned casting stations for all wind directions, in addition to the banks. The fishing season is usually 28 March to 19 October inclusive. There is a large fishing hut, complete with easy chairs, and picnic facilities. Owner is Andrew Joynson, telephone: Dolton 371/363. From 28 March telephone: Dolton 360.

Meldon
Natural Trout Fishery

A 54-acre lake close to Okehampton. Fly and bait fishing for brown and rainbow trout. Spinning is also permitted. Season 15

March to 30 September inclusive.

Times: Sunrise to one hour after sunset. There is no bag limit but fish must be over 7 in. Warden is Harry De Quick. Telephone: Tavistock 3705.

Burrator
Natural Trout Fishery

One of the most picturesque reservoirs in Britain, **Burrator's** 150 acres being surrounded by Dartmoor's hills and Forestry Commission woodland. Very popular with walkers and people just out to enjoy nature at its very best. The lake is 13 miles from Plymouth.

Offers zoned fly-fishing and spinning for natural brownies, and brook and rainbows stocked in the fry stage. Very big brown trout hunt the deeps, the record standing at well over double figures. Such a wild fish fights like no other, and is the experience of a fishing lifetime. Burrator's season is 15 March to 30 September inclusive, and you can fish from sunrise to midnight. Bag limit is four fish over a minimum of 7 in. Boats are available on day of fishing only, not bookable in advance. Robin Armstrong is the warden. Telephone: Yelverton 2564.

Venford
Natural Trout Fishery

A 33-acre lake near Ashburton, for spinning and bubble float fly-fishing. Brook and brown trout stocked as fry. Bait and traditional fly-fishing is not permitted. The season is 15 March to 12 October. Fishing times: one hour before sunrise to one hour after sunset. Bag limit five fish   7 in. minimum size. Warden is David French.

Avon Dam
Natural Trout Fishery

It's a fair walk from the car-park to the 50-acre lake but not a hardship as the path follows a Dartmoor River of incredible beauty, the water continuously plunging over granite ledges and rocks on its journey to the sea. Offers zoned spinning and fly-fishing for brown and brook trout, also worm fishing between 15 March and 12 October. Fishing times are one hour before sunrise to one hour after sunset.

There is no bag limit but fish must be over 7 in. Graham Stickland is the warden. Telephone: South Brent 2230.

Bellbrook Valley Trout Fishery

I had the pleasure of casting the first fly, and declaring these waters open, two years ago. There are five good ponds to fish set in a heavily wooded valley, several miles west of Tiverton off the road to Rackenford. It is not a big fish water, but the quality of sport is excellent.

Season is 1 May to 31 October. Owner is Major John Braithwaite. Telephone: Oakford 292. A 24-hour answering service is available for bookings.

CORNWALL
Siblyback

Certainly the most popular trout reservoir in Cornwall, due to its close proximity to Plymouth, and several other large towns. Catch figures show well over 12,000 brown, rainbow and brookies are taken each season, the local record being a rainbow in excess of 12 lb.

Siblyback's 140 acres is high on the edge of Bodmin Moor, and somewhat open to the elements. Mist is a nuisance, at times, but is more than compensated for by marvellous dawns and sunsets. Early-morning and evening fishing is especially good.

General facilities at the reservoir are excellent and include a large snack-bar. Water sports, such as sailing, wind surfing, water-skiing and canoeing are under the control of the Lake's Recreational Centre. Enquiries should be addressed to: The Membership Secretary, Siblyback Lake, Common Moor, Liskeard. A great variety of birds visit the area and watching enthusiasts have the benefit of a hide with identification charts.

Fishing times are one hour before sunrise to one hour after sunset. Bag limit five fish over 10 in. Season: 1 April to 12 October inclusive. Boats are available but not on Thursdays or Fridays.

Useful Flies: Black lures, Baby Doll, Brown Muddler, Invicta, Beefeater.

Argal

A 65-acre water close to Falmouth stocked with rainbow, brown, and brook trout. The season is 1 April to 12 October inclusive, but the reservoir normally remains open for winter rainbow fishing until Christmas Eve.

The bag limit is five fish over 10 in. but any fish caught between 7 and 10 in. while making the bag may be retained. Fishing times are one hour before sunrise to one hour after sunset. Boats are not available on Thursdays and Fridays. Argal's resident warden is: Bob Evans, Little Argal Farm, Budock Penryn. Telephone: 72544.

Argal and Stithians Trout Fly Fishing Club run events and have a boat available at Stithians Reservoir.

Useful Flies: Black lures, Baby Doll, Grey Dun, Invicta, Orange Muddler.

Porth

A small but very popular water of 40 acres near the busy holiday town of Newquay. Traditional fly-fishing for brown, brook and rainbow trout between 1 April and 12 October, bag limit five fish over 10 in. Fishing times between one hour before sunrise to one hour after sunset. Boats for two persons are available on day or half-day basis. (Not Tuesday or Wednesday.)

Porth is a very good area for the keen bird-watcher and permits covering the period of 1 April to 31 March are available from the resident warden Dennis Parkyn. Porth reservoir telephone: Newquay 2701.

The lake is used by the Newquay sailing club on Sundays only. Porth reservoir fly-fishing club has its headquarters at the lake.

Useful flies: Baby Doll, Silver Doctor, Black Gnat, Black and Peacock Spider.

Stithians
Natural Trout Fishery

A 274-acre water near Helston, which offers fly-fishing for natural brown trout and brook and rainbow trout, stocked out in the early days of their development. In keeping with other natural fisheries this is no bag limit, but fish must be a minimum of 7 in.

The season is 15 March to 13 October inclusive. Fishing times one hour before sunrise to one hour after sunset. Nigel Vogwill is the warden. Telephone: Truro 3541.

Useful flies: Baby Doll, Invicta, Mallard and Claret.

Crowdy

115 acres of water near Camelford in north Cornwall. Offers zoned fly and bait fishing for natural brownies, rainbow and brook trout stocked in the fry stage.

No bag limit, minimum size 7 in. Season 15 March to 12 October inclusive. Times: one hour before sunrise to one hour after sunset. Warden is Francis Bartlett, telephone: Camelford 3396.

Upper Tamar

The boundary between Cornwall and Devon runs through the middle of the 81-acre lake. Being within easy driving distance of Bude, Bideford and Holsworthy, it's a catchment area for a great many anglers, which is borne out by the 12,000 or so rainbow, brown and brook trout taken each year.

The water record for rainbow stands at just over double figures and the average catch is 1.7 fish per rod day. **Upper Tamar's** resident warden is Ken Spalding, Sparrapark, Upper Tamar Lake, Kilkhampton. Day tickets can be purchased at his residence.

Fishing times are one hour before sunrise to one hour after sunset between 1 April – 12 October. Fishing boats can be booked in advance or if you want to take a chance, on the day of fishing. No boats on Thursdays. Upper Tamar Lake has an active fishing club, who put on numerous events throughout the year.

Useful flies: Mallard and Claret, Blue Dun, Brown & White Nymph, Green Nymph, Sweeney Todd, Black Fly.

SOMERSET & DORSET
Clatworthy

One of two upland waters on the edge of Exmoor, offering first-class fishing in magnificent surroundings. **Clatworthy** is approximately 130 acres stocked with rainbow and brown trout. As with all Wessex Authority Reservoirs only fly-fishing is allowed, the season being 4 April to 15 October. Bag limit three brace of takable-size fish (12 in.). Boats are available. Season permits can be purchased at the Wessex Fisheries and Recreation Department, Bridgwater House, Bridgwater, Somerset. Daily bank permits are available from a self-service kiosk at the lake.

Further information will be supplied by Reg Deer. Telephone: Wiveliscombe 23549.

Otterhead Lakes

Two waters of approximately two acres, previously part of a magnificent landscaped country estate in the Blackdown hills, eight miles south of Taunton. Nature has now taken back what was hers, and one can fish in a most attractive and slightly unusual setting.

Fly-fishing from the banks is permitted between 4 April and 15 October, bag limit three brace of takable fish (12 in.). The lakes are regularly stocked with brownies and rainbows.

Permits can be purchased from a self-service kiosk at the lake, or the Fisheries and Recreation Department, Wessex Water Authority, Bridgwater House, Bridgwater, Somerset.

Hawkridge

A very picturesque water of 32 acres nestling in a small valley in the Quantock Hills, six miles west of Bridgwater. Brown and rainbow trout are stocked, the daily bag limit being three brace of fish, minimum size 12 in. Fishing season is 29 March to 15 October inclusive from the banks only. A kiosk for self-service day permits is sited at the eastern end of the lake. Hawkridge has an active sailing club.

Durleigh

This is a well-established trout fishery set in rural surroundings not far from Bridgwater. It is a lowland water of 77 acres holding excellent brown and rainbow trout. Both bank and boat fly-fishing is available between 24 March and 15 October. Three brace of fish, minimum size 12 in., is the daily bag. All the usual facilities including a self-service permit kiosk. Bob Jones: Telephone Bridgwater 424786 will be pleased to give further information.

Sutton Bingham

A 142-acre water four miles south of Yeovil, under the control of the Wessex Water Authority. It's a most attractive fishery set in lovely rolling countryside on the Somerset/Dorset border. The reservoir is regularly stocked with rainbow and brown trout, the daily bag being three brace of takable-size fish (12 in.). Boat fishing is available.

Season 29 March to 15 October inclusive. Permits from a self-service kiosk. Further information can be obtained from Peter Hill, telephone: Yetminster 872389.

A sailing club operates on the lake.

RIVER GAME FISHING

The western counties are rich in unpolluted rivers and there is first-class fishing for salmon and sea trout. Most of the best stretches are privately owned, but the South-west Water Authority have the rights to part of the River Exe, on the outskirts of Exeter, and the River Lyn, close to Lynton and Lynmouth. Day permits are very reasonably priced to which must be added the cost of a water licence.

Sea trout fishing is also good at many places, particularly on the Taw and Torridge in North Devon, where the water is sufficiently coloured to allow daylight fishing. Popular flies for taking this attractive and hard-fighting fish include mallard, teal blue and claret. Although by no means complete, the following list gives some indication of river game fishing available in Devon and Cornwall.

River Exe
Salmon brown trout. Countess Weir area: Contact Exeter and District Angling Association Secretary, 57 Woodwater Lane, Exeter, Devon.

River Dart
Salmon, sea trout, brown trout. East and west from junction to Wallabrook and from Pizwell to junction of East Dart River. Right bank of West Dart from Huccaby Bridge to Dartmeet. Contact: L. S. Mutton, The Duchy Office, The Square, Princetown, Devon.

River East Lyn
Salmon, brown trout, sea trout. Lynmouth to Watersmeet to Rockford Bridge. The stretch boasts 17 named pools. Contact: SWWA, 3/5 Barnfield Road, Exeter, Devon.

River Teign
Brown trout. Twelve miles of both banks. Chagford Bridge area. Contact: The Upper Teign Fishing Association, W. L. Young, The Old Rectory, Drewsteignton, Devon.

Devon's River Exe is a noted water for salmon fishing.

River Torridge

Salmon, sea trout, brown trout. Three-quarters of a mile above and below Dipper Mill Bridge. One mile between Sheepwash and Black Torrington Bridge. Contact: R. A. Stewart, The Devilstone Inn, Shebbear, Devon.

River Taw

Salmon, sea trout, brown trout. Three and a half miles of fishing downstream from Umberleigh Bridge. Contact: M. A. F. Tate, The Rising Sun, Umberleigh, North Devon.

River Tavy, Walkham, Plym, Meavy

Salmon, sea trout and brown trout. Many miles on both banks of each river. Contact: D. Giles, Woodcote, Crapstone, Devon.

River Otter

Brown trout. Weston Bridge upstream. Contact: L. Stevenson, Otter Inn, West, Nr Honiton, Devon.

Fowey

Salmon, sea trout. Lanhydrock two miles. Season and Day permits. Contact: The Secretary, Lanhydrock Angling Association, The National Trust, Estate Office, Lanhydrock Park, Bodmin, Cornwall.

Tamar

Salmon, sea trout, brown trout. Launceston 1½ miles. Limited number of half and full rods available to members of Launceston Angling Association. Restricted to fly and artificial bait only. Contact: M. R. Jones, 3 Penance Terrace, Windmill Hill, Launceston, Cornwall.

Leaflets on salmon fishing, seasons, etc, are available from the South-west Water Authority, 3/5 Barnfield Road, Exeter, Devon.

In the area covered by the Wessex Water Authority, salmon and sea-trout fishing is restricted to the chalk streams of the Avon and Dorset divisions, where the Hampshire-Avon, Dorset-Frome and River Piddle provide some of the most spectacular sport to be found in Southern England.

Excellent trout fishing is to be found in the upper reaches of the major rivers, such as Dorset-Frome, River Piddle, Nadder Allen and Wilys. Although all are strictly preserved by riparian owners, limited fishing is available to the visiting angler. In Somerset the upper reaches of the Rivers Brue, Parrett, Tone and Isle provide good sport.

Clubs and syndicates with interests in these waters are fully listed in the Wessex Water Authority's leaflet on game fishing, available from: 2 Nuffield Road, Poole, Dorset.

COARSE FISHING

This has taken a dramatic upward swing in the West country over the past few years, and there are now excellent facilities throughout the region.

SOMERSET

Natural river systems and numerous man-made channels drain the Somerset moorlands and provide a wealth of coarse fishing. The principal fisheries are the Rivers Brue, Parrett, Yeo, Axe, Tone, Kings Sedgemoor Drain and the Huntspill, this latter water being the scene of many top-class competitions, including a National Championship.

One also has the choice of the Avon and Kennett Rivers, and the Bridgwater/Taunton Canal, all of them being in the top echelon of coarse waters.

The season in the Wessex Authority region is 16 June – 14 March. Species inhabiting the rivers and canals include rudd, chubb, dace, carp, tench and pike.

The North Somerset Association of Anglers, comprising Weston-super-Mare and District AC, Highbridge Angling Association, and the Clevedone & District Freshwater AA control a great amount of river, pond and drain fishing. Secretary is D. Kenwood, 90 Slade Road, Portishead, telephone: 8947, who will be pleased to forward an informative leaflet covering every aspect of the Association's varied activities, and a detailed run-down on 12 waters: Make sure you enclose a SAE.

If your preference is stillwater coarse fishing two excellent waters are run by the Wessex Authority.

Pallington Lakes

A 7-acre complex of a coarse fishing pond and two trout lakes

Coarse fishing is rapidly growing in popularity and there are now many reservoirs and lakes offering good sport with carp, roach, tench, rudd, perch and bream.

not far from Dorchester. Regular stocking with bream, carp, roach, tench and perch, including specimen fish, ensures the water provides consistent sport. The season is 16 June – 14 March, fishing times 8.00 a.m. to one hour after sunset. Permits can be purchased from a self-service kiosk. Facilities at Pallington include toilets, an excellent car-park and picnic area. For further information telephone: Poole 71144.

Canford Pond

This caters for disabled fishermen, and platforms conveniently positioned along a causeway are approached by an easy path. Organised parties of anglers confined to wheelchairs can fish free of charge, providing arrangements have been made with the Wessex Divisional Fisheries and Recreation Officer, telephone: Poole 71144.

Canford Pond is on the outskirts of Little Canford, not far from Wimborne. Permits are issued on a 'season only' basis, but half-price season tickets can be purchased by senior citizens and registered disabled.

Information on all charges and fishing permits can be obtained from the following Wessex Authority Offices: Avon/Dorset Division, 2 Nuffield Road, Poole, Dorset, telephone: Poole 71144.
Somerset Division, P.O. Box 9, King Square, Bridgwater, Somerset.
Bristol/Avon Division, Key House, P.O. Box 95, The Ambury, Bath.
The Authority publish a complete list of all coarse-fishing clubs active in the counties of Somerset, Dorset, Hampshire and Wiltshire. An invaluable guide for every fisherman interested in coarse fishing.

DEVON

Exeter Canal

The water has a large population of perch, rudd, roach, tench, eels, carp and pike, fishing being permitted along its whole length of six miles between the Basin and Turf. A most popular spot for winter sport is undoubtedly the maritime basin, where fishing takes place against the background of the famous nautical museum which has a fascinating collection of ships of all shapes and sizes from across the centuries.

In times of flood on the adjacent River Exe and during very cold snaps, fish are quick to find refuge in the Basin, where the water is always several degrees warmer. The popularity of the spot, which offers not only excellent fishing but plenty of shelter from boats parked on hardstandings, does, however, lead to intensive angling activity, and Exeter's thinking men are constantly preaching the message that every fish must be handled with extreme care.

The canal has a big head of pike, 40 having been taken in a day at Double Locks. Some match-men would like to see them culled, but an equal number of noncompetitive fishermen hold a different view, believing that nature should be allowed to take its own course.

Full details for fishing the canal and 15 other waters run by the Exeter & District Angling Association from: D. Beavan, 46 Hatherleigh Road, Exeter, Devon.

Grand Union Canal

Fishing on this picturesque waterway is restricted to the part between Tiverton and Foss End Bridge, Burlescombe.

Excellent sport can be had with tench, rudd, roach, carp and pike. For full details contact: The County Estates Surveyor, County Hall, Exeter, Devon, telephone: 77977 or local tackle shops.

Rackerhayes Ponds

Five lakes controlled by the Newton Abbot Fishing Association are stocked with bream, carp, roach, perch, tench and pike.

Day tickets for visitors can be purchased at tackle shops in the Newton Abbot, Torquay and Paignton areas. Secretary is A.

Preston, 1 Balmoral Close, Newton Abbot, Devon.

Slapton Ley

The largest natural freshwater lake in the West country, separated from the open sea only by the width of a road, and Slapton Beach.

The 200-acre water holds an excellent head of rudd, perch, roach and pike. Many of the largest predators have been caught by dead and live baiting near the thick bank of tall reeds on the southern edge, approximately 300 yards from the inlet where the field centre's fleet of ten rowing boats are moored.

Craft can be hired for a day or half-day at very reasonable prices. (Maximum three anglers to a boat.) Advanced bookings are taken on Slapton 466. Landing nets come with the boat, but you must have your own tackle and bait.

Slapton is situated between Dartmouth and Kingsbridge, and there is plenty of accommodation in the immediate vicinity. The Ley attracts a great variety of wildlife, and is the perfect spot for nature lovers.

Barnstaple

Barnstaple and District Angling Association issue day tickets for Venn Pond and part of Bestridge Pond only. The waters contain most species of coarse fish, and local tackle shops sell visitor's permits.

Alder Quarry Pond

A privately owned 4½-acre lake eight miles to the east of Launceston, on the Okehampton Road. Excellent fishing for perch, tench, bream and carp, in picturesque surroundings. There is excellent self-catering accommodation available, the facilities including a swimming pool. Tackle can be hired, and bait is usually available. For bookings contact: R. Westlake, Alder

Farm, Lewdown, Okehampton, telephone: Lewdown 241.

Lower Tamar Lake

This is a 51-acre mixed trout and coarse fishery near Kilkhampton operated by the South-West Water Authority. Three years ago the water received a massive injection of crucian carp, which have settled down really well.

Common carp also inhabit the water, and fish up to 20 lb are frequently taken. Rudd and tench have always been lively feeders at Lower Tamar, and bags in excess of 50 lb have been made. Lower Tamar is looked after by Ken Spalding, telephone: Kilkhampton 262.

Carp may not be retained in keep nets.

CORNWALL
College

This water of 38 acres near Penryn and Falmouth was the subject of much-heated discussion when the SWWA changed its status from a pure trout fishery to a mixed coarse and trout fishing water. Now the furore has died down, both sections of the angling community are enjoying good sport, and the lake is a very popular venue indeed. College is open for fishing all year round, as there is no coarse fishing 'close' season in Cornwall.

Stocked fish include many hundreds of carp to nearly 15 lb in weight. All coarse fish must be returned to the water, but four trout over 7 in. may be kept.

Fishing times are one hour before sunrise to one hour after sunset.

Bob Evans is the Resident Warden, Little Argal Farm, Budock, telephone: 72544 (Penryn).

Wheal Grey Pool

It's at Ashton on the main Penzance to Helston Road. One of the best-stocked private coarse lakes in Cornwall. Holds common, mirror and crucian carp, to a weight of 16¼ lb, also bream, tench, perch and rudd, which run to specimen size. There is no close season.

Contact: Dave Burn, West Cornwall Angling Centre, Hale, telephone: 754292.

The water is under the control of Marazion Angling Club who hold weekly matches.

Tindeen Fishery

Three 1-acre lakes close to Penzance. One is fully matured and holds three species of carp, while the others have recently been improved and restocked with rudd, roach, perch, tench, bream and dace.

Day, weekly and season tickets are available. Contact: G. J. Laity, Bostrase, Gold Sithney, Penzance, telephone: Germoe 3486.

Bude Canal

Two miles of water are controlled by the Bude Canal Angling Association. There is excellent fishing for roach, rudd, perch, tench, dace and eels. Large carp are also frequently caught.

Although there is no close season in Cornwall, the Association do not allow fishing on the canal between 1 April and 31 May inclusive. Secretary: B. Putt, 2 Orchard Close, Poughill, Bude.

A recent netting and transfer operation, prior to lowering the water for repairs to the lock gates, gave a graphic indication of the water's fishing potential. Over a period of three days many thousands of fish, including carp of 13 lb and specimen perch and roach, were trapped.

Stone Lake

A 4½-acre water, eleven miles east of Launceston on the A30.

Holds bream, roach, perch, common and crucian carp. Night fishing is not allowed. Accommodation and food is available at Stone Farm.

Contact: W. P. Ponsford, Stone Farm, Bridestowe. Telephone: 253. An illustrated brochure will be sent on request.

Dutson Water

A good lake close to Launceston, holding common and crucian carp, tench, rudd and perch. Accommodation on a self-catering basis is available. Certified location for Caravan Club Members.

Contact: E. J. Broad, Lower Dutson Farm, Launceston, telephone: 2607.

INDEX